MW00674828

This catalogue designed by The Anderson Galleries
Composition and Press-work by
B. H. Tyrrel, New York

SALE NUMBER 2161
PUBLIC EXHIBITION FROM SUNDAY, APRIL SEVENTEENTH

IMPORTANT
SPANISH, FRENCH & ITALIAN
WORKS OF ART

DATING FROM THE XVth
TO THE XVIIIth CENTURY

FURNITURE, SCULPTURES
NEEDLEWORK, TEXTILES
ART OBJECTS IN SILVER
BRONZE & IRON

SOLD BY ORDER OF

DANIEL H. FARR COMPANY
15 EAST 57TH STREET
NEW YORK

TO BE SOLD AT UNRESERVED PUBLIC SALE
THURSDAY, FRIDAY, SATURDAY AFTERNOONS
APRIL TWENTY-FIRST, TWENTY-SECOND, TWENTY-THIRD
AT TWO O'CLOCK

THE ANDERSON GALLERIES
[MITCHELL KENNERLEY, President]
489 PARK AVENUE AT FIFTY-NINTH STREET, NEW YORK

1927

CONDITIONS OF SALE

ALL BIDS TO BE PER LOT AS NUMBERED IN THE CATALOGUE.

The highest bidder to be the buyer. In all cases of disputed bids the decision of the Auctioneer shall be final.

Buyers to give their names and addresses and to make such cash payments on account as may be required, in default of which the lots purchased shall be resold immediately.

Purchases to be removed at the buyer's expense and risk within twenty-four hours from the conclusion of the sale, and the remainder of the purchase money to be paid on or before delivery, in default of which The Anderson Galleries, Incorporated, will not be responsible for any loss or damage whatever, but the lot or lots will be left at the sole risk of the purchaser, and subject to storage charges.

All lots will be placed on public exhibition before the date of sale, for examination by intending purchasers, and The Anderson Galleries, Incorporated, will not be responsible for the correctness of the description, authenticity, genuineness, or for any defect or fault in or concerning any lot, and makes no warranty whatever, but will sell each lot exactly as it is, WITHOUT RECOURSE.

If accounts are not paid and purchases removed within twenty-four hours of the conclusion of the sale, or, in the case of absent buyers, when bills are rendered, any sum deposited as part payment shall be forfeited, and The Anderson Galleries, Incorporated, reserves the right to resell the lot or lots by either private or public sale, without further notice, and if any deficiency arises from such resale it shall be made good by the defaulter, together with all expenses incurred. This condition shall be without prejudice to the right of this Company to enforce the sale contract and collect the amount due without such resale, at its own option.

The Anderson Galleries, Incorporated, will afford every facility for the employment of carriers and packers by the purchasers, but will not be responsible for any damage arising from the acts of such carriers and packers.

The Anderson Galleries makes no charge for executing orders for its customers and uses all bids competitively, buying at the lowest price permitted by other bids.

A Priced Copy of this Catalogue may be obtained for One Dollar
for each Session of the Sale

THE ANDERSON GALLERIES, INC.

489 PARK AVENUE AT FIFTY-NINTH STREET, NEW YORK

TELEPHONE REGENT 0250   CATALOGUES ON REQUEST

SALES CONDUCTED BY MR. F. A. CHAPMAN, MR. A. N. BADE AND MR. E. H. L. THOMPSON

DANIEL H. FARR COMPANY

ANTIQUE WORKS OF ART

PHILADELPHIA
2141 LOCUST STREET
PALM BEACH
COUNTY ROAD

15 EAST 57ᵀᴴ STREET
NEW YORK, N.Y.

March Seventh
1 9 2 7

Anderson Galleries,
Park Avenue & Fifty Ninth Street,
New York City.

Gentlemen:

Having lately decided to discontinue our Palm
Beach branch we are consigning to you, for un-
restricted public sale, our collection of Spanish,
French and Italian furniture, textiles and objects
d'art dating from the XV to the XVIII Centuries.

Those interested in searching for rare pieces
abroad know the difficulties of obtaining genuine
examples on account of the ever growing scarcity
and we feel that the opportunity offered to the
public in this sale is an unusual one.   We guar-
antee the authenticity of the various lots offered.

Yours very truly,

Daniel H Farr

DHF:O

ORDER OF SALE

FIRST SESSION

NUMBERS 1-145

FURNITURE AND MISCELLANEOUS SMALL OBJECTS

NUMBERS 1-50

1 VALENCIAN GLAZED POTTERY TILE SPANISH, 17TH CENTURY
Inscribed "Plaza Real" with crown, amorini and foliage above.
Painted in cobalt-blue on white ground. Chipped.
Size, 13½ x 11½ inches

2 TWO TALAVERA POTTERY PLATES SPANISH, 17TH CENTURY
Painted in blue and orange on a cream ground; one representing an
archaic bird and foliage, the other an armorial cartouche. (2)
Diameter, 9¾ x 8½ inches

3 SIX VALENCIAN PAINTED POTTERY TILES
SPANISH, 17TH CENTURY
Representing archaic birds in circular medallions. Painted in blue,
orange and brown. (6)   *Size, 6 inches square*

4 PAIR OF VALENCIAN POTTERY PHARMACY JARS
SPANISH, 17TH CENTURY
Painted with figures of ladies and foliage scrolls in cobalt-blue on
white ground. (2)   *Height, 10½ inches*

5 WALNUT RELIQUARY BOX SPANISH, 17TH CENTURY
The hinged lid and sides carved with geometrical ornament and
rosettes in low relief. Has the original wrought iron hinges, handle
and lock.   *Size, 11½ x 7 inches*

1.

6 SMALL CARVED AND GILDED MIRROR

SPANISH, EARLY 18TH CENTURY

The rectangular frame carved in high relief with borders of foliage.

Size, 14½ x 11¾ *inches*

7 SMALL WALNUT BENCH   SPANISH, CIRCA 1700

With finely turned legs and stretchers. The top covered in antique flowered silk brocade.   *Height,* 15 *inches; width,* 24 *inches*

8 SMALL WALNUT BENCH   SPANISH, CIRCA 1700

Nearly similar to the preceding.

9 SMALL WALNUT SIDE TABLE   SPANISH, 17TH CENTURY

With four pleasing spool-turned supports braced by plain stretchers. Fitted in front with a panelled drawer.

Size of top, 30½ x 18½ *inches*

10 CARVED WALNUT CHAIR OF SGABELLO TYPE

SPANISH, 17TH CENTURY

Cartouche-shaped back, panelled seat and tapered and flaring supports.

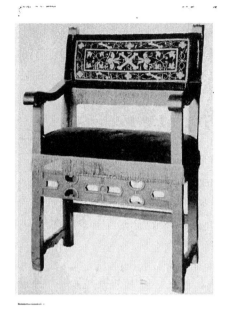

[11]

11 WALNUT AND VELVET ARMCHAIR

SPANISH, MID-17TH CENTURY

With slightly curved and scrolled arms, plain square supports and pierced front stretcher. The low rectangular back mounted with a panel of Renaissance silk-embroidered crimson velvet with metal fringe. Crimson velvet seat.

[SEE ILLUSTRATION]

3

12 **WALNUT SPINDLE-BACK CHAIR**   SPANISH, CIRCA 1700
With open arcaded back, solid seat and turned front supports with stretchers.

13 **SMALL CARVED AND PAINTED MIRROR**
                     SPANISH, 18TH CENTURY
The narrow upright frame shaped at the top and base and crested by a carved open shell.   *Size,* 20½ x 7½ *inches*

14 **SMALL WALNUT SPINDLE-BACK CHAIR**
                     SPANISH, 17TH CENTURY
The arcaded open back, supports and stretchers carved with scale walnut. Panelled seat.

15 **PAIR OF WROUGHT STEEL AND BRASS ANDIRONS**
                     ITALIAN, 17TH CENTURY
The tall tapered pillars capped by brass ball finials. Standing on handsome scrolled and splayed bases. (2)   *Height,* 30 *inches*

16 **PAIR OF STEEL ANDIRONS**   SPANISH, EARLY 18TH CENTURY
The slightly tapered pillars ornamented with conventional leafage and standing on splayed bases. (2)   *Height,* 17 *inches*

17 **LEATHER-COVERED WALNUT ARMCHAIR**
                   SPANISH, EARLY 17TH CENTURY
The back and seat mounted with panels of hand-tooled leather designed with rows of grotesque animal and bird forms and floral motifs. Bordered with large circular metal bosses. Plain arms and square supports.

18 **LEATHER-COVERED WALNUT ARMCHAIR**
                   SPANISH, EARLY 17TH CENTURY
Of nearly similar type to the preceding.

[19]

19 CARVED WALNUT SIDE TABLE SPANISH, EARLY 17TH CENTURY
The rectangular top, slightly overlapping at either end, is fitted with
one drawer carved with geometrical ornament and flanked by fluted
pilasters. On sturdy columnar supports braced by plain stretchers.
ball feet.   *Height, 32 inches; size of top,* 41 x 22 *inches*
From a private collection in Granada.

[SEE ILLUSTRATION]

20 CARVED AND GILDED WOOD STATUETTE
FLEMISH, 17TH CENTURY
Standing figure of St. Catherine holding emblem of her martyrdom.
Height, 19 *inches*

[SEE ILLUSTRATION]

5

21 PAINTED AND CARVED RELIQUARY BOX

SPANISH, 16TH CENTURY

Carved in relief on four sides with large amorini heads painted and gilded. (As is)   *Height, 6½ inches; width, 7 inches*

22 WALNUT CENTRE TABLE WITH IRON BRACE

SPANISH, 17TH CENTURY

On lyre-shaped end supports of handsome scroll form with turned iron stretchers. Overlapping rectangular top.

Size of top, 51 x 30 inches

23 WALNUT CHEST   SPANISH, 17TH CENTURY

An interesting medium-sized coffer with the original wrought iron lock and hasp and corner clamps. The front carved with strongly conventionalized floral medallions.

Height, 16 inches; width, 44 inches

24 SMALL CARVED AND GILDED VITRINE

SPANISH, 18TH CENTURY

Wall cabinet for a statuette of the Holy Virgin, outlined with carved sprays of foliage and flowers, the interior painted with landscape and trees. Charming piece.   *Height, 27 inches; width, 17 inches*

25 PAIR OF CARVED AND GILDED WOOD CANDLESTICKS

SPANISH, 17TH CENTURY

With baluster stems, wide circular bobèches and shell-carved triangular baroque bases. (2)   *Height, 20 inches*

26 WALNUT AND CUT VELVET BENCH   SPANISH, 17TH CENTURY

Top covered in crimson cut velvet with silk fringe. Vase-turned supports and stretchers.   *Height, 15 inches; width, 26 inches*

[27]

27 CARVED RENAISSANCE CASSONE

NORTH ITALIAN, EARLY 16TH CENTURY

The front richly carved in the Milanese style of high Renaissance, showing processions of allegorical figures in panels framed by borders of arabesque scrolls, grotesque animal forms and figures of saints standing in tabernacles. With handsome pierced lock of wrought brass.

From Coomb Abbey. Similar examples are in the Rijke Museum, Amsterdam; and the South Kensington Museum, London.

Height, 22 inches; length, 5 feet 9 inches; width, 21½ inches

[SEE ILLUSTRATION]

7

28 CARVED AND GILDED WOOD HANGING LANTERN

ENGLISH, 18TH CENTURY

Hexagonal, with arched glass panels. High dome and turned side pilasters with moulded and dentilled capitals. Electrified.

From Reigate Priory. *Height, 31 inches*

29 PAIR OF SMALL BRASS CANDLESTICKS

SPANISH, 18TH CENTURY

With slender baluster stems and circular bases. (2)

Height, 5 inches

30 CARVED AND GILDED SMALL MIRROR

SPANISH, 18TH CENTURY

The rectangular frame coated with gesso carved and gilded.

Size, 15½ x 14 inches

31 WALNUT SIDE TABLE WITH IRON BRACE

SPANISH, 17TH CENTURY

Oblong top on lyre-shaped end supports strengthened by gracefully curved iron rails. *Size of top, 56 x 19½ inches*

32 CARVED WALNUT ARMCHAIR SPANISH, LATE 16TH CENTURY

Showing Gothic influence. The fluted supports braced by pierced and carved front stretchers. The seat and back mounted with panels of hand-tooled leather.

33 VELVET-COVERED WALNUT ARMCHAIR

SPANISH, EARLY 17TH CENTURY

In severe Renaissance style. The rectangular back and the seat mounted with panels of purple silk velvet with gold galloons and fringe. Slightly curved arms and pierced front stretcher.

8

[34]

34 HAND-PAINTED AND PANELLED DOOR

VENETIAN, LATE 18TH CENTURY

In the Louis XVI taste. Panelled with shaped moulding which
frames still-life groups, painted in subdued colors, surrounded by
posies of summer flowers in brighter colors on a light background.
The reverse with similar flowers and fruits, in the manner of Jean
Simeon Chardin. *Height, 5 feet 11 inches; width, 33 inches*

[SEE ILLUSTRATION]

9

35 PAINTED AND CARVED DOOR   VENETIAN, 18TH CENTURY
In the Louis XVI taste. Painted light blue with yellow borders.
Panelled with shaped mouldings, the lower part occupied by raised
acanthus rosettes; the upper part glazed. Original iron trefoil hinges
and lock.   *Height, 6 feet 8 inches; width, 3 feet 4½ inches*

36 WALNUT ONE-DRAWER SIDE TABLE   SPANISH, 17TH CENTURY
On four baluster-turned supports with plain stretchers. Fitted in
front with one moulded drawer. Slightly overlapping top.
      Size of top, 31½ x 22½ inches

37 SMALL TURNED WALNUT TABOURET   SPANISH, 17TH CENTURY
On slightly raked and turned supports. Overlapping top.
      Height, 19 inches; width, 20 inches

38 CHILD'S SMALL WALNUT VARGUENO   SPANISH, 17TH CENTURY
Fitted with three drawers with spiral bone colonnades painted and
gilded. Interesting piece. Stands on small turned feet.
      Height, 11½ inches; width, 17 inches

39 CARVED AND PAINTED WOOD MODEL OF MAN-OF-WAR
      SPANISH, 18TH CENTURY
Fully rigged three-masted vessel without sails. The hull painted
yellow and black and showing twenty-two guns. The pointed bow
embellished with the lion of Castile. Set into cradled stand.
      Height, 35 inches; length, 36 inches

**40 RARE WROUGHT IRON AND VELVET ECCLESIASTICAL
CHAIR**   ITALIAN, 16TH CENTURY
Cathedral chair of a high church dignitary. With curved X-shaped
frame. The four corner posts capped by large ball and baluster
finials of gilded bronze, chased with the arms of a cardinal. Seat
cover and cushion of antique red velvet with yellow silk and metal
thread galloons and fringe. Several of these important cathedral
chairs are illustrated in Schottmuller, "Wohnungskultur and Möbel
der Italienischen Renaissance". *Height, 30 inches; width, 27 inches*

[SEE ILLUSTRATION]

10

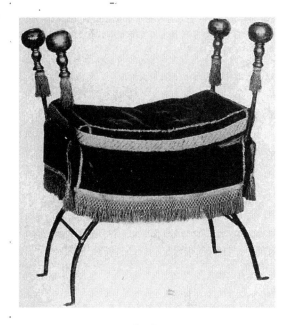

[40]

41 HAND-HAMMERED COPPER KETTLE SPANISH, 17TH CENTURY
With rounded body, slightly tapered cylindrical neck and wide loop
side handles. Adaptable as jardinière or log scuttle.

Height, 15½ inches; width, 22 inches

42 PAIR OF BRASS AND IRON ANDIRONS SPANISH, CIRCA 1700
Handsome baluster pillars with ball finials. Scrolled and splayed
bases embellished with cartouche shields. (2) *Height, 17 inches*

43 PAIR OF SMALL PAINTED TIN LANTERNS
SPANISH, 18TH CENTURY
Triangular shape, with pierced and domed top. Painted red and
fitted for electricity. (2) *Height, 19 inches*

11

44 **OIL PAINTING ON PANEL**   SPANISH, 17TH CENTURY
Depicting a company of musketeers and halberdiers who have taken
possession of a fortified town, the surrender of which is being effected
by a group of town officials and soldiers seen in the foreground. On
cradled panel. Carved and gilded baroque frame.
Purchased from Durlacher Brothers.   *Size, 18½ x 25¼ inches*

45 **PAIR OF BRASS ALTAR CANDLESTICKS**
                                           SPANISH, 18TH CENTURY
Pleasing pair with baluster shaped stems and wide square tray
bases. (2)   *Height, 6½ inches*

46 **CARVED AND GILDED WOOD ALTAR CABINET**
                                      SPANISH, EARLY 18TH CENTURY
Composed of a pair of small cupboards with star pattern doors inset
with colored glass; a cornice and four spiral fluted columns. Painted
with coats-of-arms. Adaptable as small built-in cupboards. (As is)

47 **LOUIS XVI MAHOGANY COMMODE**   FRENCH, 18TH CENTURY
Of three drawers furnished with gilt bronze ring handles. Fluted
corner pilasters extending into short tapered and turned supports.
Mottled antique Sienna marble top.
                     Height, 35 inches; width, 37½ inches

48 **FOUR TURNED WALNUT SIDE CHAIRS**   SPANISH, CIRCA 1700
The open rectangular backs contain four slender spool-turned upright spindles between horizontal rails. Handsome turned posts;
solid seats. (4)

49 **FOUR WALNUT SPINDLE-BACK SIDE CHAIRS**
                                           SPANISH, 17TH CENTURY
Of nearly similar type to the preceding chairs. (4)

50 **WALNUT CENTRE TABLE WITH IRON BRACE**
                                           SPANISH, 17TH CENTURY
On handsome scrolled end supports of lyre form strengthened by
ornamental curved iron rail. Rectangular top.
                     Length, 55 inches; width, 22 inches

POLYCHROME AND SCULPTURED WOOD FIGURES

51 **PAINTED AND CARVED WALNUT RELIEF PANEL**

SPANISH, 16TH CENTURY

Representing a motif of the high Renaissance, an amorino head in profile. Finely carved, painted and gilded. Rare.

Height, 25 inches; width, 12 inches

52 **SMALL CARVED AND POLYCHROME RELIEF PANEL**

'SPANISH, 16TH CENTURY

Representing a figure of the Madonna wearing rich vestments, standing under an architrave. Painted and gilded.

Height, 15¾ inches; width, 8 inches

53 **CARVED AND POLYCHROME FIGURE OF A KING**

SPANISH, LATE 17TH CENTURY

Seated figure wearing a crown and holding missal in left hand. His garments richly painted and gilded. *Height, 19½ inches*

54 **CARVED AND POLYCHROME WOOD STATUETTE**

FRENCH, 15TH CENTURY

Kneeling figure of a female Saint wearing rich draperies and headdress, her hands clasped in attitude of prayer. Traces of polychromy and gilding. Rare and interesting early carving, probably of the Burgundian School. *Height, 11½ inches*

55 **CARVED AND POLYCHROME WOOD COAT-OF-ARMS**

SPANISH, EARLY 17TH CENTURY

Displaying a pointed shield charged with a sceptre and tree, ensigned by a plumed visor and flanked by two lions rampant. Surrounded by boldly carved scrolls. Motto and inscription, "Laus Deo-Armas de Los Articas de Artibar". *Height, 26½ inches; width, 18½ inches*

56 **CARVED AND POLYCHROME WOOD STATUE**

SPANISH, 17TH CENTURY

Standing figure of St. Lorenzo wearing richly gilded and painted dalmatica and holding a missal. A wide circular nimbus surmounts his head. The figure stands upon a carved and gilded wood plinth of hexagonal form, which bears the name of the Saint.

Height with plinth, 27½ inches

[57]   [58]

57 CARVED AND POLYCHROME STATUE OF ST. BARBARA

FLEMISH, CIRCA 1500

Voluminously draped standing figure of the Saint, holding an open
book in her left hand. Her hair falls in graceful folds about her
shoulders, her other garments are leaf gilded, the borders show
traces of polychromy simulating embroidery. At the back are incised the "four finger" Flemish hand-marks. The figure stands upon
a pentagonal plinth of somewhat later date. An exceedingly interesting early figure with every characteristic of a Flemish master
wood sculptor. Purchased from Stora, Paris. *Height, 16½ inches*

[SEE ILLUSTRATION]

58 GOTHIC POLYCHROME AND CARVED STATUE

SPANISH, 15TH CENTURY

Standing figure of St. Peter with his emblems. Carved in characteristic Flemish Gothic style. The outer garments richly painted and
gilded with floral arabesques, have acquired a fine mellow patina.
From a private collection in Madrid. *Height, 19¾ inches*

[SEE ILLUSTRATION]

14

[59]

59 **BRONZE MORTAR**   FLEMISH, DATED 1666
With concave sides, flaring rim, and slightly rounded base. Chiselled
with the following inscription: "Bartholomews cauthals me fudit
ano MDCLXVI Adrianus de Vadder." Stands on a moulded circular
oak plinth. From a private collection in Hasselt.

Height, 13 *inches; diameter,* 14½ *inches*

[SEE ILLUSTRATION]

15

60 TWO BRONZE LION FINIALS   SPANISH, 16TH CENTURY

Seated Flemish Gothic lions, one with octagonal base, the other with spherical base. Rare. (2)   *Height, 6¾ inches*

61 BRONZE MORTAR   SPANISH, 17TH CENTURY

Decorated with coats-of-arms and pilasters in relief. The flaring rim with a band of star ornament.

From the Sir John Laking Collection.

Height, 3½ inches; diameter, 5 inches

62 BRONZE BELL   SPANISH, CIRCA 1700

Convent bell with moulded flaring rim and trefoil-shaped handle.

Height, 8¾ inches

63 TWO SMALL BRONZE BELLS   FLEMISH, 17TH CENTURY

Embellished with bands of inscriptions and floral motifs in low relief. Interesting specimens. (2)   *Height, 3½ and 5 inches*

64 SMALL BRONZE BELL   FLEMISH, 16TH CENTURY

Decorated with festoons and flowers in relief, the border with inscription, handle formed of three cherubs. Border inscribed, "Sit Nomen Domini Benedictum".   *Height, 4½ inches*

FURNITURE

65 DECORATIVE RED LACQUER WORK BOX
SPANISH, 18TH CENTURY

Gilded with Chinoiserie and foliage on ground of brilliant red lacquer.

Size, 14 x 10 inches

66 CARVED AND PAINTED MIRROR IN THE BAROQUE TASTE
SPANISH, 18TH CENTURY

Carved with acanthus leaves and flowers in high relief, and gilded. Background painted a dark tone.

Height, 29 inches; width, 27½ inches

67 SMALL WALNUT MARQUETRY BENCH
SPANISH, 17TH CENTURY

Rectangular top inlaid with arabesques. Splayed trestle supports with wrought iron brace. *Height, 14 inches; width, 15½ inches*

68 WALNUT FOLDING TABLE WITH IRON BRACE
SPANISH, 17TH CENTURY

On carved and hinged trestle supports of simple form. Braced by iron rails. Hinged to fold up. Oblong top with iron corner mounts.

Length, 41 inches; width, 20 inches

69 CARVED AND GILDED LOUIS XVI TRUMEAU MIRROR
Upright moulded frame with carved beaded borders. Mounted with a painted canvas panel displaying a pleasing pastorale of Watteau figures in a landscape. *Height, 5 feet; width, 27 inches*

70 TURNED WALNUT SMALL BENCH COVERED WITH SILK BROCADE
ITALIAN, 17TH CENTURY

The supports and stretchers handsomely turned in ball and ring pattern; the top covered in flowered pink silk brocade of a later date.

Height, 15½ inches; width, 31 inches

71 TURNED WALNUT SMALL BENCH COVERED WITH SILK BROCADE
ITALIAN, 17TH CENTURY

Similar to the preceding. *Height, 15½ inches; width, 31 inches*

17

72 CARVED AND PANELLED WALNUT DOOR FROM RIOJA

SPANISH, LATE 16TH CENTURY

Occupied by seventeen large and small chamferred and raised panels.
Interestingly carved in naturalistic manner with bird forms, jardinières of flowers, rosettes and arabesque scrolls.

From a convent in Rioja.   *Height, 6 feet 3 inches; width, 38 inches*

[73]

73 CARVED WALNUT AND OAK SIDE TABLE   ·

SPANISH, 17TH CENTURY

Richly carved on all sides with bold acanthus motif in high relief,
and fitted with two drawers. Turned and tapered columnar supports
with moulded flat stretchers and ball feet. The top slightly overlaps
at either end.

From a private collection in Madrid.

Length, 5 feet 10 inches; width, 26 inches

[SEE ILLUSTRATION]

18

74 **THIRTY-SEVEN RENAISSANCE PAINTED FRIEZE PANELS
FROM MODENA**   NORTHERN ITALIAN, 16TH CENTURY
Each painted with the bust of a warrior in profile under a Renaissance arch, which is supported by fluted capitals. The spandrels of
the arches are filled with leaf arabesques. Painted in subdued colors
upon a dark ground.

These extremely interesting small oblong panels formed part of a
long frieze in a palace near Modena, Italy, and show traces of having
been scorched by fire. (37)

Approximate size of each, 17½ x 9 inches

75 **PAIR OF BRASS CANDLESTICKS**   SPANISH, 18TH CENTURY
With turned baluster stems and wide square tray bases. (2)

Height, 7 inches

76 **PAIR OF BRASS CANDLESTICKS**   SPANISH, 18TH CENTURY
Nearly similar to the preceding. (2)   *Height, 6 inches*

77 **VELVET-COVERED MANTILLA BOX**   SPANISH, 18TH CENTURY
Oblong, with rounded ends. Gilded bronze lock and handle. Covered
in crimson velvet with gold galloon.

Length, 29 inches; width, 12½ inches

78 **WALNUT SIDE TABLE WITH TWO DRAWERS**
                                    SPANISH, 17TH CENTURY
The front carved in an unusual geometrical design and slightly
scrolled. Overlapping top. Sturdy ring and ball turned supports
and side stretchers strengthened by turned slender brace placed at
an angle.

From Estremadura.   *Length, 4½ inches; width, 27½ inches*

19

ONE OF TWO WALNUT ARMCHAIRS
SPANISH, SEVENTEENTH CENTURY

[79]

79 TWO WALNUT ARMCHAIRS COVERED IN PINK SILK

SPANISH, LATE 17TH CENTURY

With handsomely moulded and scrolled arms, supports and stretchers. The arched and slightly canted backs and the seats covered in antique pink silk with silver and gold wide galloons and shaped silk fringe. (2)

From a private collection in Madrid.

[SEE ILLUSTRATION]

20

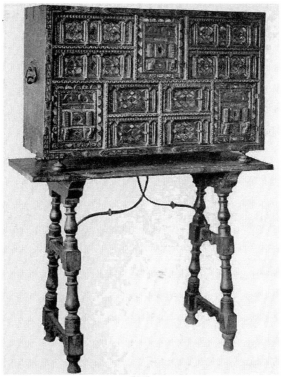

[80]

80 **INLAID AND CARVED WALNUT OPEN VARGUENO ON
STAND**   SPANISH, EARLY 17TH CENTURY
A highly decorated cabinet. Fitted with eight drawers and three
lockers, including smaller drawers and covers. The front simulating
miniature porticos inset with painted bone plaquettes of mosaic form
and faced with spiral pilasters. The borders mounted with plaques
and rosettes of wrought metal. On stand with slightly splayed and
turned supports and iron braces.
From a private collection in the Province of Zamora.

Height, 5 feet; width, 42 inches

[SEE ILLUSTRATION]

21

81 SCULPTURED MARBLE CAPITAL FROM GRANADA
COPTIC, 9TH TO 11TH CENTURY

The sides covered with carved Coptic characters. An interesting example of early Arabic sculptured stone work, purchased from a private collection in Granada. *Height, 15 inches; width, 14½ inches*

82 PAIR OF BRASS AND IRON ANDIRONS
SPANISH, 18TH CENTURY

With bold baluster shaped pillars. (2)   *Height, 17 inches*

83 PAINTED AND CARVED BEDSTEAD   SPANISH, CIRCA 1780

In the French taste. The headboard, supported by slightly tapered and marbled columns, is incised, painted and gilded with a representation of the Temple of Flora under a drapery canopy. Full size. With box spring and hair mattress.

84 SMALL OAK STOOL   SPANISH, 17TH CENTURY

With oblong moulded top, plain columnar supports and heavy stretchers.   *Height, 23 inches; width, 12½ inches*

85 CARVED AND GILDED WOOD PANELLING FROM A HIGH
ALTAR   SPANISH, LATE 17TH CENTURY

Occupied by six upright panels carved in high relief with rich decoration of acanthus leaves and scrolls. The pilasters with amorini heads beneath composite capitals. The deep moulded cornice with interesting scratch-carving of sportsmen and landscapes, marine subjects and foliage arabesques. Heavy leaf gilding. Hinged and forming a three-fold screen. *Height, 5 feet 5 inches; length, 8 feet 6 inches*

22

[86]

86 REPOUSSE TIN LANTERN   SPANISH, 18TH CENTURY
Square, with glass sides and high dome, handsomely decorated with
repoussé panels of conventional flowers and foliage, centered by
gilded medallions of the Holy Lamb.
From the Cathedral of Zamora. *Height, 42 inches; width, 15 inches*

[SEE ILLUSTRATION]

87 REPOUSSE TIN LANTERN   SPANISH, 18TH CENTURY
Similar to the preceding.
From the Cathedral of Zamora.

88 WALNUT AND DAMASK ARMCHAIR   SPANISH, 17TH CENTURY
A pleasing chair of French design. The rectangular back and seat
covered with antique golden-yellow silk damask with red, white and
yellow silk fringe. Ring-turned supports and stretchers, slightly
curved arms.

23

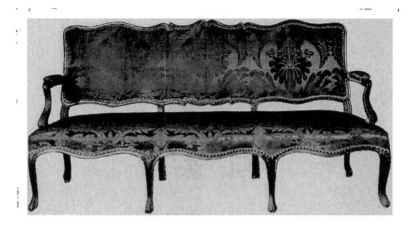

[89]

89 **DAMASK-COVERED AND GILDED SETTEE IN THE LOUIS XV**
TASTE   SPANISH, 18TH CENTURY
The serpentine back and seat covered in antique crimson silk damask
with jardinière pattern. Slightly voluted arms and cabriole supports.

Length, 6 feet

[SEE ILLUSTRATION]

90 **WALNUT CENTRE TABLE**   ·   SPANISH, 17TH CENTURY
Medium size, with slightly overlapping oblong top. On scale-carved,
boldly scrolled end supports with twisted iron cross brace.

Size of top, 3 feet 9½ inches x 25½ inches

91 **CARVED AND GILDED BAROQUE MIRROR**
                               SPANISH, LATE 17TH CENTURY
The rectangular frame richly carved in high relief with scroll acanthus and open shells.   *Height, 27 inches; width, 23 inches*

24

[92]

92 CARVED WALNUT CENTRE TABLE

SPANISH, EARLY 17TH CENTURY

Two sides magnificently carved with sprays of acanthus foliage and grapevine in relief. The ends with large rosette medallions. Fluted and raised stiles. Three drawers on one side. Stands on four unusual turned columnar legs partly carved with fluting and braced by moulded square stretchers. Four feet restored. Massive slightly overlapping top.

From a collection in Madrid.   *Length, 6 feet; width, 28 inches*

[SEE ILLUSTRATION]

25

93 **TURNED WALNUT SMALL BENCH** SPANISH, 17TH CENTURY
The rectangular top covered in flowered yellow silk trimmed with
colored silk fringe. *Height, 13½ inches; width, 27 inches*

94 **WALNUT CENTRE TABLE WITH TWO DRAWERS**
SPANISH, 17TH CENTURY
The frame all around finely carved with rosette and shell medallions,
and fitted with two drawers at one side. Slightly overlapping oblong
top. Sturdy ring-turned supports with moulded heavy stretchers.
From a private collection in Llanes, a town in Northern Spain, situ-
ated on the route of pilgrimage to the shrine of Santiago de Com-
postela. *Length, 6 feet 6 inches; width, 23 inches*

95 **WALNUT ARMCHAIR COVERED IN SILK FLOWERED
BROCADE** SPANISH, LATE 17TH CENTURY
With handsome voluted and grooved arms terminating in scrolls.
Vase and ring turned supports and stretchers. Arched back and
seat covered in antique flowered silk brocade.

96 **WALNUT AND DAMASK ARMCHAIR** SPANISH, 17TH CENTURY
A handsome chair with boldly voluted and scrolled arms, vase and
ring turned supports and stretchers. The high back and seat covered in jardinière pattern crimson silk damask with red and gold
fringe.

97 **LEATHER-COVERED WALNUT STOOL** SPANISH, 15TH CENTURY
On four chamferred supports with cross stretchers. Circular top
covered in dark leather and studded with brass nails.
Height, 21 inches; width, 12 inches

98 **WALNUT CENTRE TABLE** SPANISH, EARLY 17TH CENTURY
Rectangular, with two handsomely carved drawers on either side.
On bold shaped end trestle supports braced with scrolled iron stretchers. The drawers embellished with handsome pierced iron escutcheons. From Burgos. *Length, 4 feet 9 inches; width, 28½ inches*

99 **FIVE WALNUT CHAIRS WITH ARCADED BACKS**
SPANISH, 17TH CENTURY
Pleasing dining chairs with panelled seats. The open backs are arcaded and crested by carved scrolls. The front stretchers shaped
to harmonize with the back. Fitted with loose seat cushions covered
in figured crimson silk damask. (5)

SPANISH WROUGHT IRON WORK

100 GILDED AND WROUGHT IRON APPLIQUE

SPANISH, 17TH CENTURY

Wall light from a church in Soria, of foliated scroll form with wide circular bobèche. Rare. *Length, 25 inches*

101 IRON TRIPOD TORCHERE SPANISH, 16TH CENTURY

With wide circular bobèche, twisted stem and tripod base. Rare. *Height, 52 inches*

102 GOTHIC WROUGHT IRON TRIPOD CANDLESTICK

SPANISH, LATE 15TH CENTURY

Very rare specimen. With pricket top and tripod triangular supports twisted in rope pattern.

Obtained from a private collection in Madrid. Nearly similar examples are illustrated in Galdacano catalogue, "Exposicion de Hierros Antiquos Españoles". Similar examples are also to be seen in Cau Ferrat Museum at Sitges near Barcelona. *Height, 35½ inches*

103 IRON WINDOW GRILL SPANISH, 18TH CENTURY

With vertical, spirally twisted and partly balustered rails. *Height, 3 feet 6 inches; width, 4 feet 5 inches*

104 LEAD CISTERN ENGLISH, DATED 1776

Ornamented with figures of amorini, angels and animals, flanking a jardinière of flowers. Adaptable as jardinière. Some defects. Rare. *Height, 16 inches; length, 33 inches; width, 10 inches*

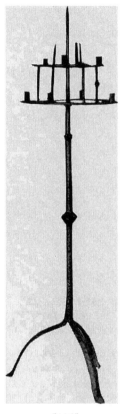 

[106]　　　　　　　　　　　　[105]

105　**IRON TRIPOD TORCHERE**　　　　SPANISH, LATE 16TH CENTURY
A fine specimen with balustered standard, wide ·circular fluted
bobèche and pierced candle socket. On fluted tripod base.

Height, 43 inches

[SEE ILLUSTRATION]

106　**GOTHIC IRON TORCHERE**　　　　SPANISH, EARLY 16TH CENTURY
With two-tier circular top for ten candle lights. Slightly tapered
standard on tripod base. Rare.　　　.　*Height, 5 feet 6 inches*

[SEE ILLUSTRATION]

28

107 **IRON BALCONY**   SPANISH, 17TH CENTURY
Large reja with vertical banisters embellished at the centres with
quatrefoil ornament. Pleasing window grill with simplicity of line.
Height, 3 feet 6 inches; length, 7 feet 5 inches; depth, 3 feet

108 **THREE PAIRS OF WROUGHT IRON FINIALS**
                                      SPANISH, 17TH CENTURY
Decorative motifs of pierced spherical form on tapered sockets. (6)
Height, 12 and 15 inches

109 **SIX IRON LATCHES**   SPANISH, 17TH CENTURY
Of different handsomely shaped scroll designs with the original bar
hasps. (6)

110 **IRON KNOCKER**   SPANISH, 16TH CENTURY
Oval shape, fashioned with two archaic lizard forms symmetrically
arranged around the curve of the knocker. Rare.   *Width, 6 inches*

111 **IRON DOOR KNOCKER**   SPANISH, 17TH CENTURY
Looped baluster shape, with original shank.

29

TEXTILES

NUMBERS 112-145

112 THREE PANELS OF FIGURED YELLOW SILK DAMASK

SPANISH, 18TH CENTURY

With bold jardinière pattern of large flowers and scrolled leaves in two shades of golden-yellow. Composed of eight strips of about three yards each. *Total length about* 24 *yards*

113 PANEL OF FIGURED CRIMSON SILK DAMASK

SPANISH, 18TH CENTURY

Patterned with bold flower leaf medallions. Composed of four strips, each three and one-quarter yards long.

Total length about 13 *yards*

114 FLOWER-EMBROIDERED BLUE SILK VIRGIN'S ROBE

SPANISH, 18TH CENTURY

Triangular shape, with beautiful sprays of roses on slender meandered stems forming a trellis pattern. In soft rose colors on ground of pale blue. Rich galloons of gold thread. Fine quality.

Width, 10 *feet; length,* 9 *feet*

115 LONG STRIP OF RUBY-RED VELVET SPANISH, 17TH CENTURY

Fine deep color and condition with braided borders.

Length, 13 *feet; width,* 21 *inches*

116 LONG STRIP OF RUBY-RED VELVET SPANISH, 17TH CENTURY

Similar to the preceding. *Length,* 13 *feet; width,* 21 *inches*

117 LONG STRIP OF RUBY-RED VELVET SPANISH, 17TH CENTURY

Similar to the preceding. *Length,* 13 *feet; width,* 21 *inches*

118 BEDSPREAD OF YELLOW FIGURED SILK DAMASK

SPANISH, 18TH CENTURY

With gold jardinière pattern of flowers and leaves. Composed of four strips joined and bordered with pleated valances.

Size, 6 *feet* x 7 *feet*

118A PANEL OF FIGURED CRIMSON SILK DAMASK

SPANISH, 18TH CENTURY

Composed of two strips of four yards each. Fine silver lace galloon. Slightly worn.

30

DETAIL OF SILK AND GOLD
EMBROIDERED STRIP
OF FIVE ORPHREYS

[119]

119 **FINE SILK AND GOLD EMBROIDERED STRIP OF FIVE
ORPHREYS**   ITALIAN, 16TH CENTURY
Showing figures of the Apostles in five circular medallions, sur-
rounded by rich Renaissance grotesques and foliated arabesques.
Finely embroidered in colored silks and heavy gold thread. Linen
lined.   *Length, 5 feet 9 inches; width, 10 inches*

[SEE ILLUSTRATION]

31

120 **PAINTED SILK BEDSPREAD**   SPANISH, LATE 18TH CENTURY
White silk charmingly painted with birds and butterflies among
delicate flower vines framing a centre large floral medallion. In
soft pastel colors. Colored silk fringe. Slightly worn.

Size about 8 *feet* x 7 *feet*

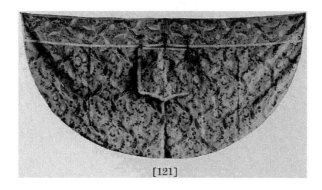

[121]

121 **SILVER AND SILK BROCADE COPE**   SPANISH, 17TH CENTURY
With all-over design of gracefully curved leaf fronds and roses in
silver thread and red silk upon a rose-pink ground. With the original hood; fine silver galloons. Linen lined.   *Width about* 9 *feet*

[SEE ILLUSTRATION]

122   FLOWERED GREEN SILK BROCADE PANEL

SPANISH, 18TH CENTURY

With brilliant jade-green ground designed with richly meandered flower vines in colored silks. Fine quality.

Size about 6 feet 6 inches square

123   **RED SILK DAMASK BEDSPREAD**   SPANISH, 18TH CENTURY

Bold flower and leaf design in two shades of red. Pleated border on three sides.   *Size about 7 feet 6 inches x 8 feet 6 inches*

124   **CRIMSON SILK DAMASK BEDSPREAD** SPANISH, 18TH CENTURY

Designed with bold flowers and scrolled leaves in two shades of brilliant red. Cut and pleated border on three sides.

Size about 7 feet 6 inches x 6 feet 6 inches

125   **BLUE SILK DAMASK PANEL**   SPANISH, 18TH CENTURY

With semi-conventionalized small flower and leaf design in two shades of medium blue.   *Size about 8 feet 6 inches x 6 feet 6 inches*

126   **BLUE SILK DAMASK PANEL**   SPANISH, 18TH CENTURY

Similar color to the preceding panel, but with small floral pattern.

Size about 7 feet square

127   **BLUE SILK DAMASK BEDSPREAD**

SPANISH, EARLY 19TH CENTURY

With bold flower and leaf design in two shades of pale blue. Blue silk braided border.   *Size about 9 feet square*

128   **BLUE SILK DAMASK BEDSPREAD**   SPANISH, 18TH CENTURY

Designed with large palmettes of flowers and leaves.

Size about 8 feet x 7 feet

129   **SMYRNA WOOL RUNNER**   17TH CENTURY

With rich conventionalized flower design in brilliant red, blue and softer shades. (As is)   *Size about 5 feet x 2 feet 6 inches*

130   **TWO CUSHIONS**

One covered in antique green silk damask with silver galloon; the other in flowered and striped pink silk brocade. (2)

Width about 18 inches

131 **PANEL OF RED SILK BROCADE**   SPANISH, 18TH CENTURY
Fine quality. All-over design of flower posies on meander stems in colored silk and gold thread. On red ground.
Size, 7 feet 6 inches x 34 inches

132 **EMBROIDERED VELVET AND DAMASK TABLE RUNNER**
SPANISH, 17TH CENTURY
Altar scarf composed of two panels of ruby velvet embroidered with floral wreaths and small urns in colored silk. The centre of crimson damask with palmette design. Linen lined.
Size, 7 feet 11 inches x 23 inches

133 **PANEL OF FIGURED CRIMSON SILK DAMASK**
SPANISH, 18TH CENTURY
Consisting of three and a half breadths of about two and a quarter yards each.

134 **LARGE NEEDLEWORK SAMPLER**
SPANISH, EARLY 19TH CENTURY
Richly worked with bands of diaper ornament framing small bird, flower and domestic objects and alphabets. On old linen.
Size, 28 x 22 inches

135 **SILK CHALICE COVER**   SPANISH, 18TH CENTURY
With large exotic flowers on salmon-pink ground. Silver thread openwork border.   *Size, 22 inches square*

136 **GREEN AND GOLD SILK BROCATELLE TABLE COVER**
SPANISH, 17TH CENTURY
Designed with rich baroque foliage in pale gold on bright green ground. Narrow fringe.   *Size, 6 feet x 3 feet 9 inches*

137 **GOLD AND SILK BROCADE CHASUBLE**
SPANISH, 18TH CENTURY
Designed with Chinoiserie foliage scrolls and figures in gold thread on salmon-pink ground. Yellow silk galloons. Worn.

138 **TWO PANELS OF FLOWERED PINK SILK**
SPANISH, 18TH CENTURY
Designed with sprigs of exotic flowers in turquoise, yellow, and black on a salmon-pink ground. (2)   *Size, 6 feet x 34 inches*

34

139 **GREEN SILK DAMASK PANEL** SPANISH, 18TH CENTURY
With naturalistic flowers and leaves in two shades of emerald-green.
Size about 8 feet x 3 feet 6 inches

140 **TWO EMBROIDERED RED VELVET CHAIR SEATS**
SPANISH, 18TH CENTURY
Rich design of bold floral arabesques embroidered in bright colored
silks on a ruby velvet ground. Embroidery of later date. (2)
Size about 23 x 21 inches

141 **TWO EMBROIDERED RED VELVET CHAIR SEATS**
SPANISH, 18TH CENTURY
Similar to the preceding. (2) *Size about 23 x 21 inches*

142 **TWO TABLE STRIPS** SPANISH, 17TH CENTURY
Piece of red and gold silk brocade; piece of red and gold cut velvet.
Worn. (2) *Length, 34 and 50 inches; width about 22 inches*

143 **CRIMSON VELVET TABLE MAT** SPANISH, 17TH CENTURY
Centre with appliquéd silk embroidery of coat-of-arms of earlier
date. Gold galloon. *Size, 30 x 23 inches*

144 **PAIR OF GOLD-EMBROIDERED PRIEST'S COLLARS**
SPANISH, 16TH CENTURY
Embroidered with cardinal's arms and arabesques on cloth-of-gold
ground. (2) *Width, 23 inches*

145 **THREE SILK TABLE MATS** SPANISH, 18TH CENTURY
Flower-embroidered chalice cover; blue and silver brocaded mat;
striped blue and white silk mat. (3) *Width about 22 inches*

SECOND SESSION

NUMBERS 146-288

FURNITURE AND SMALL OBJECTS

NUMBERS 146-191

146 **TWO VALENCIAN POTTERY PHARMACY JARS**

SPANISH, 17TH CENTURY

Painted with archaic birds and foliage. (2) *Height, 12 inches*

147 **GLAZED POTTERY TILE** SPANISH, 17TH CENTURY

Finely painted with representation of the Christ with the Cross. Framed by a border of formal flowers. Painted in colors. Rare.

Size, 11 inches square

148 **TALAVERA PAINTED POTTERY TAZZA**

SPANISH, 17TH CENTURY

Decorated with a male bust portrait surrounded by foliage in green and yellow on cream ground. *Diameter, 8½ inches*

149 **PAIR OF GLAZED TALAVERA POTTERY JARS**

SPANISH, 18TH CENTURY

Decorated with buildings, trees and landscapes in cobalt-blue on a white ground. Fine quality. (2)

Height, 7¼ inches; diameter, 10½ inches

150 **WALNUT STOOL** SPANISH, 16TH CENTURY

Sturdy piece with chamferred and slightly raked supports and solid octagonal top. *Height, 20 inches; width, 10½ inches*

151 **CARVED AND GILDED RELIQUARY BOX**

SPANISH, 16TH CENTURY

With domed lid and panelled sides. Decorated with floral arabesques in blue and gold. Original iron hinges and lock.

Height, 9½ inches; width, 9 inches

152 **CARVED SMALL MIRROR**   SPANISH, EARLY 18TH CENTURY

Decorative small mirror in the baroque taste. Frame pierced with open shell, flowers and foliage scrolls; crested by a conch shell.

Height, 30½ inches; width, 19½ inches

153 **TWO WALNUT SPINDLE-BACK CHAIRS**

SPANISH, 17TH CENTURY

(2)

154 **SMALL WALNUT TABLE**   SPANISH, 17TH CENTURY

With slightly tapered and ring-turned supports; heavy overlapping rectangular top fitted with one deep drawer.

Height, 32 inches; width, 31½ inches

155 **TALL OAK STOOL**   SPANISH, 16TH CENTURY

Sturdily built table stool with moulded top, slightly tapered columnar supports and plain stretchers. *Height, 25 inches; width, 17½ inches*

156 **SMALL WALNUT SIDE TABLE WITH ONE DRAWER**

SPANISH, EARLY 17TH CENTURY

Stands on four ring turned supports with plain stretchers. Fitted with panelled drawer with iron drop handle. Shaped apron below.

Height, 27½ inches; width, 28½ inches

38

[157]

157 TURNED WALNUT ARMCHAIR SPANISH, 15TH CENTURY
Showing French influence. The back and seat covered with figured
green silk damask with gold galloon. The legs and stretchers have
fine ring and ball turnings. Grooved and boldly curved arms. A
handsome chair.

[SEE ILLUSTRATION]

158 TURNED WALNUT ARMCHAIR SPANISH, 17TH CENTURY
Baluster turned supports and stretchers. The back and seat covered
in figured bright green silk damask.

159 PAIR OF PAINTED DIRECTOIRE SIDE CHAIRS
SPANISH, CIRCA 1800
The open backs painted with amorino and foliage arabesques in char-
acteristic subdued Directoire colors. Slip seats covered in blue silk
brocatelle.
From a palace in Majorca. (2)

39

160 **PANELLED AND CARVED PINE DOOR** SPANISH, 17TH CENTURY
With geometrical designs of small rectangular, chamferred and
moulded panels. With the original lintel and the semicircular over-
door which is filled with radiating turned balusters. (As is)

Height, 9 feet; width, 4 feet

161 **WALNUT AND GREEN DAMASK ARMCHAIR**

SPANISH, 17TH CENTURY
The high back and seat covered in antique emerald-green silk damask
with silk fringe. Bold voluted and grooved arms. Vase and ring-
turned supports with turned stretchers.

162 **WALNUT SIDE TABLE WITH TWO DRAWERS**

SPANISH, EARLY 17TH CENTURY
Standing on four handsome ring-turned legs with ball feet and plain
stretchers. Two drawers in the front panelled and with heart-shaped
key plates: Dark patina.
From Estremadura. *Size of top, 40 x 25½ inches*

[163]

163 **CARVED AND GILDED WOOD CASKET** SPANISH, 16TH CENTURY
Rectangular with domed lid. Carved in relief with animal grotesques
and foliage arabesques, and gilded. Lock missing, and worn at the
base. *Height, 9½ inches; width, 11½ inches*

[SEE ILLUSTRATION]

40

[164]

164 **FINELY CARVED WALNUT CENTRE TABLE ON SCROLL
SUPPORTS** SPANISH, EARLY 17TH CENTURY
With three drawers at one side carved with bold foliage sprays in
relief and with iron handles. The remaining three sides with bands
of thumb carving, rosette blocks at the corners. On sturdy scrolled
end supports of lyre form.

Length, 7 feet 2 inches; width, 31½ inches

[SEE ILLUSTRATION]

165 **PAIR OF BRASS ALTAR CANDLESTICKS** ITALIAN, DATED 1692
With acanthus enriched, triangular bases and paw feet. Tapered
baluster stems and circular tops. Bases engraved with the date as
above. (2) *Height, 22 inches*

166 **POLYCHROME METAL HANGING LANTERN**
SPANISH, 18TH CENTURY
Octagonal with glass sides; pierced stone top; pendent silk and gold
tassel below. *Height, 22 inches*

41

167 CARVED WALNUT COFFRET   SPANISH, 17TH CENTURY
The front and sides embellished with panels of carved geometric ornament. Domed lid with original iron lock, hasp and handle. Stands on tapered shoes.   *Height, 14 inches; width, 18½ inches*

168 PAIR OF ANDIRONS   SPANISH, 17TH CENTURY
Shaped iron pillars capped by brass baluster finials and standing on splayed bases. Accompanied by a small pair of iron ember tongs. (3)

169 SMALL WALNUT SIDE TABLE   SPANISH, 17TH CENTURY
With moulded overlapping top, spool-turned supports and plain stretchers; fitted with a one-panel drawer.   *Size, 33 x 23 inches*

170 PAIR OF WROUGHT IRON ANDIRONS SPANISH, 18TH CENTURY
The tall pillars spirally twisted and tapered; boldly splayed bases. (2)   *Height, 24 inches*

171 CARVED AND POLYCHROME SMALL MIRROR
                                     SPANISH, 18TH CENTURY
Frame painted blue and gold and carved, with borders of formal foliage in relief.   *Size, 16½ inches square*

172 PAIR OF BRASS CANDLESTICKS   SPANISH, 18TH CENTURY
With slender baluster stems and wide moulded circular bases. (2)
                                     Height, 14¼ inches

173 SMALL WALNUT BENCH   SPANISH, CIRCA 1700
With tapered and turned supports and stretchers. The top covered in green silk damask with fringe.
                         Height, 15 inches; width, 24½ inches

174 WALNUT ARMCHAIR   SPANISH, LATE 17TH CENTURY
The grooved and down-curved arms terminating in curved rosaces. Turned and tapered square supports with flattened ball feet. Slightly domed X stretchers with centre turned finials. Back and seat covered in rose-figured red silk. Unimportant restoration at back of frame.

[175]

175 CARVED WALNUT CASSONE OF THE RENAISSANCE

ITALIAN, 16TH CENTURY

The borders handsomely carved with full fluting and gadroon orna-ment. The front and top panelled with raised mouldings and em-bellished with marquetry inlay of putti in landscapes. Centre em-bellished with a handsome acanthus and scroll armorial cartouche in high relief. Carved female caryatides at the corners. Stands on lyre paw feet. Well executed repair to front moulding.

Height, 25½ inches; length, 6 feet; depth, 23 inches

[SEE ILLUSTRATION]

176 PAIR OF CARVED AND POLYCHROME WOOD ALTAR CANDLESTICKS

SPANISH, 17TH CENTURY

The baluster stems richly carved and gilded with baroque shells and scrolls. (2)   *Height, 25½ inches*

177 PAIR OF CARVED AND POLYCHROME WOOD ALTAR CANDLESTICKS

SPANISH, 17TH CENTURY

Similar to the preceding pair. (2)   *Height, 25½ inches*

43

178 **VERY FINE CARVED AND INLAID WALNUT VARGUENO ON CHEST STAND** SPANISH, 16TH CENTURY

The remarkably fine interior of small drawers and lockers carved as miniature tabernacles, the columns being of white bone, the panels outlined with leaf gilding and embellished with small bone insets of cruciform, lozenge and rosette motifs, the inlay being sparingly used. The piece was formerly used in a sacristy as a receptacle for small fabrics, fringes, etc., as the small labels on the drawers indicate. The let-down front is enriched with pierced and gilded iron mounts and the magnificent lock of arabesque form. Stands upon a chest base which contains two drawers and two cupboards carved with diamond-shaped mouldings and with fluted stiles at either side. The iron mounts are backed with crimson velvet.

From the Cathedral of Valencia.

Height, 5 feet; width, 3 feet 8 inches

[SEE ILLUSTRATION]

179 **DAMASK-COVERED WALNUT ARMCHAIR**

SPANISH, 17TH CENTURY

The slightly arched back and seat covered in antique green silk damask. Carved and scrolled arms, spool-turned supports and stretchers.

180 **CARVED AND GILDED MIRROR IN BAROQUE TASTE**

SPANISH, 18TH CENTURY

The rectangular frame richly carved in high relief with open shells and bold acanthus scrolls. Painted and gilded.

Height, 26 inches; width, 22½ inches

181 **CARVED AND PANELLED OAK DOOR**

SPANISH, EARLY 17TH CENTURY

Panelled in a geometrical design with mouldings in high relief. Cruciform centre, with carved archaic rosettes in lozenge panels. With original iron lock and hook latches. Black patina.

Height, 6 feet 2 inches; width, 39 inches

182 **MARINE PAINTING ON PANEL** SPANISH, 17TH CENTURY

Depicting a naval engagement between Spanish and Moorish vessels. Inscription and coat-of-arms below. *Size, 21½ x 19 inches*

44

FINE CARVED AND INLAID WALNUT VARGUENO
ON CHEST STAND
SPANISH, SIXTEENTH CENTURY

[178]

183 **CARVED WALNUT SHAPED COMMODE**   FRENCH, CIRCA 1770
Two drawers of serpentine form carved with shaped oblong and circular panels with bronze bail handles and cartouche escutcheons.
Scrolled skirt; short cabriole supports with scroll feet. Provincial
type.   *Height, 35 inches; width, 48 inches*

184 **CARVED AND INLAID WALNUT BUFFET**
                                    SPANISH, EARLY 17TH CENTURY
Fitted with two drawers with cupboards beneath. Front ornamented
with carved diamond-shaped mouldings centred by medallions which
bear crown cartouche keyplates. Borders finely carved with geometrical ornaments and inset with plaquettes of bone painted with
floral arabesques. Also studded with small brass rosettes. Panelled
sides with iron handles. Stands on ball-turned feet.
                                    Height, 34 inches; width, 42 inches

185 **WALNUT CENTRE TABLE WITH TWO DRAWERS**
                                        SPANISH, 17TH CENTURY
The slightly overlapping top contains two diamond-panelled doors
at one side and stands on ball-turned legs with plain stretchers.
                            Length, 4 feet 3 inches; width, 26 inches

186 **TURNED WALNUT STOOL**   SPANISH, 17TH CENTURY
With moulded oblong top and slightly raked vase and ring-turned
supports with stretchers.   *Height, 18 inches; width, 17 inches*

[187]

187   CARVED AND PAINTED SETTEE IN THE LOUIS XV TASTE
VENETIAN, 18TH CENTURY

A long bench with graceful lines. The serpentine seat frame painted
yellow and gold and carved with interesting small relief medallions
flanked by sprays of foliage. One end upholstered and covered in
contemporary floral silk lampas, the other end open and voluted.
On carved cabriole supports ending in scroll feet.
From a private collection in London.

Length, 7 feet; width, 21 inches

[SEE ILLUSTRATION]

47

[188]

188 FINELY PAINTED AND CARVED BEDSTEAD

SPANISH, EARLY 18TH CENTURY

Supported at each corner by richly carved and gilded rocaille scroll posts. The detached headboard is richly carved with baroque scrolls and crested by a domed canopy. The centre painted with two figures of saints in a rich scroll and floral cartouche in colors and gold on a gesso ground.   *Width, 5 feet 3 inches*

[SEE ILLUSTRATION]

48

189 PAIR OF CARVED AND POLYCHROME WOOD ALTAR
CANDLESTICKS   SPANISH, 17TH CENTURY
The baluster stems richly carved and gilded with baroque shells and
scrolls. (2)   *Height, 25½ inches*

190 SMALL WALNUT SIDE TABLE   SPANISH, 17TH CENTURY
Equipped with one drawer and standing on slightly tapered colum-
nar supports with stretchers. Geometrically carved front and sides.
Height, 33 inches; width, 36 inches

191 CARVED AND PAINTED ARMCHAIR
                                          SPANISH, LATE 17TH CENTURY
Handsome chair in the baroque taste, with shell-carved back, voluted
arms and cabriole supports braced by carved stretchers. Seat and
back covered in antique crimson velvet.

∴

OBJECTS IN BRONZE

NUMBERS 192-195

192 SMALL BRONZE BELL   FLEMISH, 16TH CENTURY
With relief decoration of animal and human forms. Hole in one
side. Handle formed of headless female figure.   *Height, 4 inches*

193 BRONZE LION FINIAL   SPANISH, 16TH CENTURY
In pure Gothic style, representing a seated lion of archaic form on
moulded octagonal plinth. Rare.   *Height, 5¼ inches*

194 BRONZE MORTAR   SPANISH, 17TH CENTURY
Decorated with mascarons and female caryatides in relief.
Height, 4½ inches; diameter, 6 inches

195 BRONZE MORTAR   SPANISH, 17TH CENTURY
Cylindrical, with moulded and flaring rim. Sides with decoration of
fleur-de-lis motifs in low relief. Handsome specimen.
Diameter, 6½ inches

49

SCULPTURED WOOD FIGURES

196 SMALL CARVED AND POLYCHROME RELIEF PANEL

SPANISH, EARLY 17TH CENTURY

Depicting St. Joseph with the infant Christ and emblems. Walnut painted and gilded.   *Height*, 18 *inches; width*, 10 *inches*

197 CARVED AND POLYCHROME WOOD RELIQUARY BUST OF ST. ANDREW   SPANISH, EARLY 17TH CENTURY

With his emblems. On moulded rectangular base inscribed with the Saint's name. Polychromed and gilded.

Height, 12½ *inches; width*, 9½ *inches*

198 CARVED AND POLYCHROME WOOD STATUE

SPANISH, 17TH CENTURY

Standing figure of Santa Marta holding an open missal in her left hand, with voluminous draperies richly gilded and polychromed. Standing on a pentagonal wood plinth which bears the Saint's name.

Height with plinth, 28 *inches*

199 POLYCHROME WOOD RELIEF CARVING

ENGLISH, 17TH CENTURY

Of lunette form, representing in relief the Queen of Sheba before King Solomon. In the background numerous figures bear the royal gifts, which have been transported on camels. The border represents a swag of acanthus leaves interlaced with fruits and flowers. Crested by an armorial motif comprising a pair of lions couchant and supporting a crown; below, a winged amorino head. At the bottom is carved "J. Reg. Jo. J. J2."

Height, 25 *inches; width*, 31 *inches*

[200]

200 **CARVED AND POLYCHROME WOOD STATUE OF COLUMBUS**
SPANISH, EARLY 16TH CENTURY

Engaging small standing figure of a man wearing open coat, disclosing sword at his side, and carrying a telescope in his right hand. This exceptionally interesting figure has always been regarded as a statuette of Columbus. The similarity to other portraits of the early explorer is easily seen.

From a private collection in Valladolid. *Height, 22½ inches*

[SEE ILLUSTRATION]

51

[201]

201 CARVED AND POLYCHROME WOOD COAT-OF-ARMS

SPANISH, LATE 16TH CENTURY

Displaying in a bold scroll cartouche an oval convex quartered shield charged with a lion rampant, a cross and two panels or pellets. A long pennant above bears a figure of St. Mark with the lion and cross. *Height, 36 inches; width, 21 inches*

[SEE ILLUSTRATION]

52

202 PAIR OF PAINTED AND CARVED WALNUT RELIEF PANELS
FRENCH, LATE 16TH CENTURY
Originally small doors from a sacristy, now joined as one panel.
Carved in high relief with figures of St. Roche wearing bishop's
robes, and St. Andrew crowned and carrying the cross. Other
figures in the background. Coated with a thin layer of stucco and
painted in subdued colors, which have acquired a fine mellow patina.
(2)   *Height, 30 inches; width, 25 inches*

[203]

203 CARVED AND POLYCHROME FIGURE OF THE VIRGIN AND
CHILD IN GOTHIC TABERNACLE   SPANISH, 16TH CENTURY
Pleasing small standing figure of the Holy Virgin wearing richly
gilded and painted robes and holding the Holy Infant on her left
arm. The figure stands in a pierced, carved and fluted Gothic tabernacle lined with crimson velvet of early period.
Total height, 21½ inches; width, 11 inches

[SEE ILLUSTRATION]

53

FURNITURE, SILVER AND SMALL OBJECTS

NUMBERS 204-244

204 **CARVED PINE ARMORIAL ARMCHAIR**

SPANISH, EARLY 17TH CENTURY

The rectangular back carved with a family coat-of-arms and motto "Delos Escueros". Panelled seat; gently curved arms.

205 **TWO BRASS ALTAR CANDLESTICKS** SPANISH, 18TH CENTURY

With delicate balustered stems, wide bobèches, and flaring circular bases. Almost a pair. (2) *Height about 11½ inches*

206 **TWO BRASS CANDLESTICKS** SPANISH, 18TH CENTURY

With baluster stems and octagonal bases. (2) *Height, 15½ inches*

207 **CARVED, PAINTED AND GILDED MIRROR**

SPANISH, CIRCA 1700

Rectangular frame painted a dark tone and decorated with carved and gilded foliage motifs in high relief.

Height, 33½ inches; width, 30 inches

208 **FINE CARVED AND GILDED RENAISSANCE ENTABLATURE**

SPANISH, 16TH CENTURY

From a church in Badajos. The three-quarter fluted columns are decorated with carved flower and leaf arabesques in relief. The capitals are of the composite order. These support a deep pediment with leaf, egg and dart, and dentil carved borders. The frieze is centred by an amorino head in high relief with carved birds and floral arabesques at either side in low relief. The moulded square splinths of the columns are restored.

Height, 9 feet 10 inches; width, 5 feet 6 inches

[SEE ILLUSTRATION]

54

FINE CARVED AND GILDED
RENAISSANCE ENTABLATURE
SPANISH, SIXTEENTH CENTURY

[208]

[209]

209 **TURNED WALNUT AND VELVET ARMCHAIR OF THE LOUIS XIII PERIOD** FRENCH, 17TH CENTURY

The low rectangular back and seat covered in fragments of sixteenth century crimson and gold cut velvet. Spiral turned arms, supports and stretchers; the arms terminating in carved female heads. From a private collection in Normandy.

[SEE ILLUSTRATION]

210 WALNUT CENTRE TABLE WITH TWO DRAWERS

SPANISH, EARLY 17TH CENTURY

The deep frame carved on all sides with large concave floral rosettes. Two drawers at one side with shaped keyplates and drop handles. On sturdy baluster-turned supports with ball feet and heavy flat stretchers. Top is slightly overlapping at either end.

Length, 4 feet 10 inches; width, 26½ inches

211 SILVER CONDIMENT BOX OF TREFOIL SHAPE

SPANISH, EARLY 18TH CENTURY

Charming piece divisioned for salt, pepper and sugar indicated by engraved letters on the hinged cover. Stands on small claw and ball feet. Gadroon borders. Centre fitted with nutmeg grater.

212 SMALL SILVER-GILT TABLE BELL   FRENCH, CIRCA 1790

With chiselled decoration of pendent swags of fruit and flowers. Small balustered handle. Paris mark.   *Height, 3¼ inches*

213 SMALL SILVER TRENCHER SALTCELLAR

POSEN, EARLY 18TH CENTURY

In the Louis XV taste. Of scroll form with shell-shaped hinged cover. Charming piece.   *Width, 3 inches*

214 OVAL SILVER CONDIMENT BOX SPANISH, EARLY 18TH CENTURY

The double hinged lid bordered with beaded ornament and engraved with the letters "VS". Interior with three divisions. On four lion-paw feet. Maker's mark stamped beneath. A charming piece.

Width, 3¾ inches

57

[217]   [215]   [216]   [217]

215 SILVER CHOCOLATE POT OF THE LOUIS XVI PERIOD

FRENCH, CIRCA 1790

Bulbous shape, on curved tripod feet. Leaf-enriched spout, slightly
domed lid with pivoted flower knob. Silver and pearwood handle.
Maker's mark under the base, also engraved initials "MG."

Height, 9 *inches*

[SEE ILLUSTRATION]

216 SILVER TEAPOT OF THE DIRECTOIRE PERIOD

FRENCH, LATE 18TH CENTURY

Of cylindrical form. Cover with swan knob; spout terminates in a
bird's head. Ball feet. Maker's mark under the base. Engraved
with small armorial crest. Carved ivory handle. Interior with original strainer.   *Height,* 4 *inches*

[SEE ILLUSTRATION]

217 PAIR OF SILVER CANDLESTICKS

SPANISH, EARLY 18TH CENTURY

With octagonal baluster stems, circular bobèches and moulded octagonal bases. Each with maker's mark under the base. Very fine.
(2)   *Height,* 9 *inches*

[SEE ILLUSTRATION]

58

[218]

218 POLYCHROMED TIN CHURCH LANTERN

SPANISH, 17TH CENTURY
Octagonal, with tapered base and domed top, surmounted by cruciform motifs. Richly pierced in a trellis pattern and ornamented
with scrolled acanthus leaves. Similar to the lanterns in the church
of St. Jose, Madrid.   *Height, 47 inches*

[SEE ILLUSTRATION]

59

219 **PAIR OF WROUGHT STEEL ANDIRONS** SPANISH, 17TH CENTURY
Dignified pair in the style of the Renaissance, with ringed pillars
and boldly splayed scroll bases.   (2)   *Height, 23½ inches*

220 **PAIR OF BRASS ANDIRONS**   SPANISH, 17TH CENTURY
With bold baluster pillars capped by ball finials; on splayed iron
supports. (2)   *Height, 17½ inches*

221 **VELVET-COVERED RELIQUARY BOX WITH SILVER MOUNTS**
                                        SPANISH, 17TH CENTURY
Of rectangular form, covered in crimson velvet and enriched with
rosettes and borders of chased and engraved silver. Cartouche-
shaped lock, the hasp of which is damaged.
                    Height, 7½ inches; width, 13¼ inches

222 **GOTHIC CARVED LINEN-FOLD DOOR**
                                        FRENCH, LATE 15TH CENTURY
An upright door of chaste design. Occupied by six rectangular
panels of fine linenfold carving, framed by grooved stiles; with
original wrought metal lock, hinges and latch. Rare.
                    Height, 6 feet 5½ inches; width, 37 inches

ONE OF SEVEN WALNUT
AND VELVET CHAIRS
SPANISH, EARLY EIGHTEENTH CENTURY

[223]

223 **SEVEN WALNUT AND VELVET CHAIRS**

SPANISH, EARLY 18TH CENTURY

The high backs have handsome crests of carved scrolls centred by pendent honeysuckle motifs, slightly tapered and turned side posts with turned finials. Graceful cabriole supports ending in carved hoof feet. The seats and backs covered in antique crimson silk velvet with gold galloons. Slightly curved stretchers. Fine quality.
(7)

[SEE ILLUSTRATION]

224 **WALNUT AND VELVET ARMCHAIR**
SPANISH, EARLY 18TH CENTURY
Harmonizing with the preceding chairs.

225 **TWO CARVED WALNUT CHAIRS** SPANISH, EARLY 18TH CENTURY
Low side chairs of similar design to the preceding. The back and
seat of one covered in antique green velvet with silver galloons. The
other in antique green silk damask. A charming pair. (2)

226 **VELVET-COVERED MISSALE ROMANUM WITH SILVERED
MOUNTS**
DATED 1807
Bound in crimson velvet and with handsomely foliated corner mounts
and clasps of pierced and chased silvered bronze.

227 **MUDEJAR CHEST**
SPANISH, 16TH CENTURY
Highly interesting because of the unusual incised carving with which
the piece is ornamented. The front shows circular rosette medallions flanking floral palmettes of archaic character. At the centre
below the extremely fine pierced metal lock are carved grotesque
animal forms. The top and sides also carved. Metal corner clamps,
hinges and side handles. Ball feet of later date.
Height, 21½ inches; width, 47 inches

62

[228]

228 IMPORTANT WALNUT CENTRE TABLE WITH TWO DRAWERS

SPANISH, LATE 16TH CENTURY

An unusually fine table of the Renaissance. Standing on six sturdy spiral carved columnar supports with ringed capitals. These are braced by heavy moulded stretchers. The frame is deeply moulded and carved on all sides with panels of foliage arabesques in relief. Two drawers at one side with iron drop handles and cartouche shaped keyplates. Fine natural walnut patina.

Length, 7 feet 1 inch; width, 29 inches

[SEE ILLUSTRATION]

229 **WALNUT CENTRE TABLE WITH THREE DRAWERS**

SPANISH, 17TH CENTURY

Handsomely carved on both sides with conventionalized flower sprays and rosettes. Three drawers at one side. On boldly scrolled end supports also finely carved. Some restorations.

Length, 6 feet 10 inches; width, 29 inches

230 **WALNUT WAINSCOT BENCH WITH IRON BRACE**

SPANISH, 17TH CENTURY

With long panelled feet; hinged and slightly canted back of similar depth. On baluster-turned end supports, slightly splayed and braced by wrought iron stretchers.

Length, 6 feet 1 inch

231 **IMPORTANT SET OF FIVE CHINESE PAINTED PANELS MADE FOR THE EUROPEAN MARKET** EARLY 18TH CENTURY

Large wall panels of kakemono form painted with Chinese figures, pavilions and garden scenes on paper mounted on canvas. Very fine and rare. (5)

Approximate sizes of each panel, 10 *feet* 6 *inches* x 15 *feet*
10 feet 6 inches x 5 *feet* 3 *inches*
10 feet 6 inches x 6 *feet* 8 *inches*
10 feet 6 inches x 6 *feet* 5 *inches*
10 feet 6 inches x 6 *feet* 3 *inches*

[SEE ILLUSTRATION]

ONE OF AN IMPORTANT SET OF
FIVE CHINESE PAINTED PANELS
EARLY EIGHTEENTH CENTURY

[231]

231A SMALL CARVED AND GILDED MIRROR   SPANISH, CIRCA 1700
The rectangular frame is embellished with carved acanthus leafage
in relief.   *Size, 21 x 16½ inches*

232 TURNED WALNUT LOW BENCH   SPANISH, 17TH CENTURY
The top covered in figured bright green silk damask with gold fringe.
Turned short scrolled legs and stretchers.
                            Height, 13½ inches; width, 30 inches

233 WALNUT SIDE TABLE WITH ONE DRAWER
                                          SPANISH, 16TH CENTURY
With sturdy ring-turned supports braced by plain stretchers. A
drawer in the front carved with lozenge-shaped panels and small
rosettes.   *Height, 31 inches; width, 41 inches*

234 IMPORTANT CARVED WALNUT ARMOIRE A DEUX CORPS
                                          FRENCH, 16TH CENTURY
A fine example of wood carving by a master craftsman of the Burgundian School. The upper part enclosed by two doors carved in
relief with allegorical male figures standing in leaf-enriched porticos.
The dividing pilasters with very fine male and female caryatides
carved as terminal figures in high relief. The centre is encircled by
raised and full fluted moulding. The base has two doors ornamented
with flat carving of foliage arabesques in moulded panels. Parts of
the base moulding are restored. A highly decorative cabinet with
exceptionally fine brown patina.
                            Height, 5 feet 11 inches; width, 4 feet

[SEE ILLUSTRATION]

66

IMPORTANT CARVED WALNUT
ARMOIRE A DEUX CORPS
FRENCH, SIXTEENTH CENTURY

[234]

235 **TURNED WALNUT ARMCHAIR**   SPANISH, 17TH CENTURY

With moulded and gently curved arms terminating in scrolls. Baluster turned supports and stretchers. The slightly canted high back and the seat covered in rose-figured gold silk.

236 **PAIR OF WALNUT AND VELVET SIDE CHAIRS**
                          SPANISH, EARLY 17TH CENTURY

With rectangular frames of pleasing simplicity. The backs and seats covered in antique crimson velvet with gold galloon. Front stretchers pierced and carved with geometrical ornament. (2)

237 **WALNUT SIDE TABLE**   SPANISH, 17TH CENTURY

The deep apron fitted with two drawers finely carved in a geometrical pattern. Slightly overlapping top. Handsome vase and ring-turned supports. The stretchers and stiles also finely carved. Has some unimportant restoration. *Size of top, 42 x 24 inches*

238 **WALNUT SHAPED COMMODE**   FRENCH, CIRCA 1750

Serpentine front; two long and two small drawers with fine foliated bronze key plates and handles. Slightly overlapping top. Brown patina. *Height, 31 inches; width, 44 inches*

239 **TURNED WALNUT SMALL BENCH**   SPANISH, 17TH CENTURY

Top covered in flowered buff silk. Ring-turned supports and stretchers. *Height, 16 inches; width, 23½ inches*

240 **FIVE CARVED WALNUT BANISTER-BACK CHAIRS**
                          SPANISH, CIRCA 1700

The backs contain three carved balusters between handsome rosette carved and scrolled horizontal slats. Plain square posts with acanthus scrolls. Spindle brace. Back and seat covered in flowered silk brocade. (5)

ONE OF THREE CARVED AND
PANELLED WALNUT DOORS
SPANISH, SEVENTEENTH CENTURY

[241]

241 THREE CARVED AND PANELLED WALNUT DOORS

SPANISH, 17TH CENTURY

Each door represents a severe geometrical design of small rectangles formed of slightly sunken and chamferred panels framed by raised and grooved mouldings. The stiles similarly grooved. With the original iron hinges, pierced handles and latches. Dark brown patina. Rare. (3)

Height of each door, 5 feet 10 inches; width, 35½ and 36½ inches

[SEE ILLUSTRATION]

69

241A **WALNUT FOLDING TABLE** FRENCH, 16TH CENTURY

A writing and game table with severe classic lines. Has hinged two-flap top and plain columnar supports, slightly splayed and braced by moulded stretchers.

A nearly similar table is in the Musée des Arts Decoratifs, Paris.

Length, 39 *inches; width,* 18 *inches extending to* 36 *inches*

242 **CARVED WALNUT AND VELVET BENCH**

SPANISH, LATE 17TH CENTURY

Boldly scrolled end supports braced by similarly scrolled medial stretcher. Top covered in ruby silk velvet with gold galloon.

Width, 28 *inches*

243 **NINE WALNUT SPINDLE-BACK SIDE CHAIRS**

SPANISH, 17TH CENTURY

The open rectangular backs contain six fine baluster-turned spindles upright between horizontal rails, the latter carved with narrow bands of scale ornament. Moulded and panelled seats; turned supports with stretchers. (9)

244 **LONG WALNUT CENTRE TABLE ON SCROLLED SUPPORTS**

SPANISH, 17TH CENTURY

A splendid table with mellow brown patina. Fine one-piece solid top overlapping at either end. The deep frame fitted with three drawers at one side. Richly carved with acanthus scrolls in relief and framed by mouldings. On handsome carved and scrolled end supports of lyre form.

From Burgos. *Length,* 7 *feet* 3 *inches; width,* 28 *inches*

SPANISH AND FRENCH IRON WORK

NUMBERS 245-254

245 **GOTHIC IRON CANDLESTICK**   CATALONIA, EARLY 15TH CENTURY
Rare early piece of unusual form with fluted tray base on three feet.
To hold nine small candles and a larger pricket candle. A nearly
similar specimen is illustrated in Galdacano, "Exposicion de Hierros
Antiquos Españoles".

246 **IRON GRILL**   SPANISH, 18TH CENTURY
Large window grill of simple geometrical design with spiral twisted
vertical and horizontal bars.   *Size, 5 feet 7 inches x 4 feet 9 inches*

247 **WROUGHT IRON GATE**   ANDALUSIAN, 17TH CENTURY
Rectangular shape, wrought in a rich Renaissance design of ara-
besque medallions interlaced with upright and horizontal bars.
Height, 7 feet 6 inches; width, 3 feet 7 inches

248 **IRON GATE**   SPANISH, 18TH CENTURY
Upright gate, with vertical and horizontal bars interlaced with
arabesque scrolls. The scrolled crest centred by a foliated finial.
Retains the old dark paint.   *Height, 8 feet; width, 3 feet 6 inches*

71

ONE OF THREE POLYCHROMED AND WROUGHT IRON APPLIQUES
FRENCH, SEVENTEENTH CENTURY

[249]

249 **THREE POLYCHROMED AND WROUGHT IRON APPLIQUES**

FRENCH, 17TH CENTURY

Candle light wall fixtures from a church interior. Formed as sprays of lilies and leaves supporting heavily gilded circular bobèches. Very fine and rare.

Purchased from a private collection near Nyon, on Lake Geneva. (3)

Length, 27 inches

[SEE ILLUSTRATION]

250 **WROUGHT IRON LARGE BALCONY** SPANISH, 18TH CENTURY
Rectangular with vertical rails, some with balustered centres, some
spirally twisted. Retains the old light green paint. Some defects.
Height, 3 feet 3 inches; length, 7 feet 9 inches; depth, 3 feet 6 inches

251 **POLYCHROMED IRON CHANDELIER** ITALIAN, 18TH CENTURY
A decorative hanging light fixture, with gracefully scrolled and foliated branches for eight candle lights radiating from the centre hub
of carved and gilded wood. The wide circular bobèches are also of
painted and gilded wood and from these depend tear drops; from
the centre hangs a large tassel.
Height, 42 inches; diameter, 42 inches

252 **CHISELLED IRON DOOR KNOCKER** SPANISH, 16TH CENTURY
Baluster shape, with scrolled and fluted crest. Rare specimen.
Length, 6½ inches

253 **EIGHT IRON SMALL LATCHES** FRENCH, 17TH CENTURY
Highly decorative door embellishments wrought in handsome scrolled
designs. (8)

254 **SIX IRON SMALL LATCHES** FRENCH, 17TH CENTURY
Similar to the preceding. (6)

TEXTILES AND NEEDLEWORK

NUMBERS 255-288

255 **LARGE YELLOW SILK DAMASK BEDSPREAD**
SPANISH, 18TH CENTURY
Patterned with jardinières and sprays of small flowers in two shades
of golden-yellow. Bordered with yellow openwork fringe. Composed of four strips. *Size, 9 feet x 6 feet 9 inches*

256 **FIGURED CRIMSON SILK DAMASK HANGING**
SPANISH, 18TH CENTURY
Patterned with clusters of flowers and leaves in two shades of bright
red. Composed of four strips of two and one-half yards each. Lined
with dyed linen. Totalling about 10 yards.

257 **GREEN SILK DAMASK BEDSPREAD** SPANISH, 18TH CENTURY
With bold flower and leaf design in two shades of bright green.
Pleated and cut border in slightly deeper tone.
Size about 8 feet square

73

258 VERY FINE RENAISSANCE EMBROIDERED VELVET
BALDACHINO STRIP   SPANISH, 16TH CENTURY
With ruby velvet ground finely embroidered with a cardinal's arms,
also beautiful flower and leaf volutes in silk and gold thread. Red
and gold silk fringe. Lined with crimson brocatelle.
From a church in the province of Saragossa.

Length, 11 feet 9 inches; width, 13½ inches

[SEE ILLUSTRATION]

259 VERY FINE RENAISSANCE EMBROIDERED VELVET
BALDACHINO STRIP   SPANISH, 16TH CENTURY
Similar to the preceding, embroidered with three coats-of-arms.
From a church in the province of Saragossa.

Length, 11 feet 9 inches; width, 13½ inches

260 VERY FINE RENAISSANCE EMBROIDERED VELVET
BALDACHINO STRIP   SPANISH, 16TH CENTURY
Similar to the preceding.
From a church in the province of Saragossa.

Length, 7 feet 2 inches; width, 13½ inches

261 FOUR PIECES OF PINK SILK EMBROIDERY
                                    SPANISH, 18TH CENTURY
Cape and collar and two smaller pieces, embroidered with small detached flowers in colored silks on salmon-pink ground. Silver thread
borders. Lined with yellow silk. (4)

74

VERY FINE RENAISSANCE EMBROIDERED
VELVET BALDACHINO STRIP
SPANISH, SIXTEENTH CENTURY

[258]

262 THREE RUBY VELVET POINTED VALANCES

SPANISH, 17TH CENTURY

With shaped gold galloons and heavy gold tassels. (3)

Length, 5 feet 9 inches; depth, 28 inches

263 PAIR OF RUBY VELVET POINTED VALANCES

SPANISH, 17TH CENTURY

Similar to the preceding. (2)

Length, 3 feet 6 inches; depth, 28 inches

264 RUBY VELVET POINTED VALANCE   SPANISH, 17TH CENTURY

Similar to the preceding.   *Length, 6 feet; depth, 28 inches*

265 SILVER AND SILK BROCADE VIRGIN'S ROBE

SPANISH, 18TH CENTURY

With all-over design of large flowers on richly meandered stems in silver thread on a ground of rose-pink silk. Silver open-work galloons. Worn.   *Length, 5 feet; width, 5 feet*

266 PANEL OF FLOWERED GREEN SILK DAMASK

SPANISH, 18TH CENTURY

Designed with large medallion, formal flowers and scrolled leaves.

Size about 7 feet square

267 PANEL OF RED SILK DAMASK   SPANISH, 18TH CENTURY

With slightly conventionalized flower design in two shades of red. Fine quality.   *Size about 7 feet 6 inches x 7 feet*

[268]

268 VERY FINE NEEDLEWORK HANGING OF IMPORTANT SIZE

[268]

268 **VERY FINE NEEDLEWORK HANGING OF IMPORTANT SIZE**

ENGLISH, DATED 1741

Representing on a bright blue ground a jardinière of large exotic flowers and leaves surrounded by plumaged birds in flight and pendent swags of similar flowers in rich colors. This fine composition is framed by a wide border containing large flowers and leaves linked by bold meandered scrolls in similar colors upon a slightly darker ground. Signed at the centre of the lower border "Alice Watson MDCCXLI". An extremely rare panel of early needlework in a remarkably fine state of preservation.

Height, 5 feet 7½ inches; width, 8 feet 6 inches

[SEE ILLUSTRATION]

77

269 **FLOWERED BLUE SILK DAMASK PANEL**
SPANISH, 18TH CENTURY
Size about 11 *feet* 6 *inches* x 3 *feet* 4 *inches*

270 **YELLOW SILK DAMASK BEDSPREAD** SPANISH, 18TH CENTURY
Fine quality bright yellow silk with large leaf and flower design.
Size about 7 *feet square*

271 **YELLOW SILK BROCADE BEDSPREAD** SPANISH, 18TH CENTURY
Striped yellow and white ground with meandered sprays of small
flowers and leaves in colors. Cut white silk border on three sides.
Size about 6 *feet* 6 *inches* x 5 *feet*

272 **GREEN SILK DAMASK COPE**   SPANISH, LATE 18TH CENTURY
With bold design of large baroque leaves and flowers. Yellow silk
galloons.   *Width,* 9 *feet*

273 **LARGE PANEL OF FLOWERED BLUE SILK**
SPANISH, EARLY 18TH CENTURY
Bright blue, with all-over sprays of flowers and leaves in shades of
silver.   *Size about* 7 *feet square*

274 **ANTIQUE SPANISH WOOLEN RUG**
With design of conventionalized flower forms on deep blue ground.
Bright red border.   *Size,* 5 *feet* x 28 *inches*

275 **PANEL OF FIGURED CRIMSON SILK DAMASK**
SPANISH, 18TH CENTRUY
Consisting of five strips, totalling about ten yards.

276 **PAIR OF FLOWERED CHINTZ HANGINGS**
SPANISH, EARLY 19TH CENTURY
Designed with delicate sprays of roses and leaves in natural colors
on a white ground. Lined. (2)   *Size about* 6 *feet square*

277 **FLOWERED SILK ALTAR SCARF**   SPANISH, 18TH CENTURY
With large exotic flowers in soft rose shades on pale green ground.
Narrow silk and silver thread borders.
Length, 7 feet; width, 21 inches

278 **TWO SMALL TABLE MATS**   SPANISH, 17TH CENTURY
Of silk brocade and green velvet. (2)   *Width, 21 and 12 inches*

279 **PIECE OF RUBY SILK VELVET**   SPANISH, 18TH CENTURY
Part of a cape, the border embroidered with silver sequins.
Length, 4 feet 2 inches; width, 18 inches

280 **PAIR OF YELLOW SILK DAMASK VALANCES**
SPANISH, 18TH CENTURY
With knotted yellow and white fringe. (2)
Length, 6 feet 6 inches; depth, 16 inches

281 **TWO EMBROIDERED RED VELVET CHAIR SEATS**
SPANISH, 18TH CENTURY
Rich design of bold floral arabesques embroidered in bright colored
silks on a ruby velvet ground. Embroidery of later date. (2)
Size about 23 x 21 inches

282 **TWO EMBROIDERED RED VELVET CHAIR SEATS**
SPANISH, 18TH CENTURY
Similar to the preceding. (2)   *Size about 23 x 21 inches*

283 **TWO SILK PANELS**   SPANISH, 18TH CENTURY
One piece bright blue with bold flower design; the other piece blue
and yellow, small flowers. (2)   *Size about 48 inches square*

284 **TWO EMBROIDERED PRIEST'S COLLARS**
SPANISH, 18TH CENTURY
Embroidered with floral swags in colored silks on gold and silver
ground. (2)   *Width, 22 inches*

79

285 **TWO EMBROIDERED VELVET PRIEST'S COLLARS**

With fine bullion appliqué of bold floral arabesques on ruby velvet ground. (2)   *Width, 24 inches*

286 **BLUE AND YELLOW SILK CAPE** SPANISH, EARLY 18TH CENTURY
With rich floral and scroll design in rose and soft yellow. Silver-embroidered border.   *Size, 48 x 30 inches*

287 **EMBROIDERED LINEN ALTAR COVER** SPANISH, 18TH CENTURY
Embroidered with clusters of flowers and mythological birds in black wool on cream linen. Deep openwork fringe and tassel border.
Length, 7 feet 3 inches; width, 2 feet

288 **TWO SMALL NEEDLEWORK SAMPLERS**   SPANISH, CIRCA 1800
One finely worked in colored silk cross-stitch; the other with widely spaced alphabets, numerals and objects. (2)
Width, 21 and 12 inches

THIRD SESSION

NUMBERS 289-446

FURNITURE AND SMALL OBJECTS

NUMBERS 289-331

289 **GLAZED STONEWARE WATER JAR**   SPANISH, 18TH CENTURY
Globular, with small neck and looped handle. Coated with rich moss-green glaze.   *Height, 11 inches*

290 **VALENCIAN GLAZED POTTERY TILE** SPANISH, 17TH CENTURY
Painted with cardinal's coat-of-arms in cobalt-blue upon a white ground. The glaze is worn off in places.   *Size, 15 inches square*

291 **PAIR OF VALENCIAN POTTERY PHARMACY JARS**
                                    SPANISH, 17TH CENTURY
Painted with figures of ladies and foliage scrolls in cobalt-blue on white ground. (2)   *Height, 10½ inches*

292 **VALENCIAN TURQUOISE-BLUE POTTERY TILE**
                                    SPANISH, 17TH CENTURY
Painted in black with an armorial medallion and conventionalized flowers. Mounted in wood frame.   *Size, 13 x 16 inches*

293 **LARGE POTTERY JAR ON STAND** SPANISH, 16TH-17TH CENTURY
Ovoidal shape, with moulded rim and tapered body. Standing in modern iron tripod.

81

294 SMALL POLYCHROMED AND CARVED MIRROR

SPANISH, 18TH CENTURY

Painted black and gold and carved with acanthus foliage in relief.

Size, 18 x 15 *inches*

295 SMALL TURNED WALNUT BENCH   SPANISH, 17TH CENTURY

Oblong top, covered in flower-figured salmon-pink silk. Vase and ring turned supports and stretchers. *Height,* 15½ *inches; length,* 20 *inches*

296 SMALL TURNED OAK CONVENT CHAIR

SPANISH, 17TH CENTURY

A nun's sewing chair with turned front supports and carved stretchers. The arched back and seat covered in figured crimson silk damask.   *Height,* 29 *inches*

297 SMALL WALNUT SIDE TABLE   SPANISH, 17TH CENTURY

With slightly overlapping rectangular top. Spool-turned supports with plain stretchers. Fitted with a carved drawer.

Height, 30 *inches; width,* 29 *inches*

82

[298]

298 WALNUT AND CRIMSON VELVET ARMCHAIR

SPANISH, LATE 17TH CENTURY

A chair of fine proportions, the slightly canted arched back and seat covered with antique crimson silk velvet, with borders of gold and silver thread and deep fringe. Moulded and voluted arms terminating in scrolls; boldly curved supports and stretchers.

This chair and the following chair are from the Cathedral of Jaen, near Granada, where they stood near the high altar.

[SEE ILLUSTRATION]

299 WALNUT AND CRIMSON VELVET ARMCHAIR

SPANISH, 17TH CENTURY

Of similar design to the preceding, except for a slight difference in the carving of the front stretcher.

300 **CARVED CEDARWOOD SMALL CHEST** ITALIAN, 17TH CENTURY
Coffret of engaging proportions, with compartmented interior. Richly
decorated on all sides and on the interior. The panels of Eastern
architecture, biblical and classical motifs outlined with delicate
mouldings and surrounded with fine Renaissance decoration of foliage arabesques, and jardinières of flowers in poker work. On small
turned feet.

Height, 15¼ inches; length, 30½ inches; width, 18 inches

301 **CARVED PINE TABOURET** SPANISH, CIRCA 1700
On splayed and grooved supports with carved side stretchers. Over-
lapping top with incurved corners.
From the province of Caceres.

Height, 16½ inches; width, 23½ inches

302 **OLD ENGLISH PAINTED PAPIER MACHE TEA TRAY**
CIRCA 1810
Made by Dyson & Benson, London, for the Spanish market.

Size, 30 x 23 inches

303 **POLYCHROMED TIN HANGING LANTERN**
SPANISH, 17TH CENTURY
Hexagonal, with high domed top and tapered base. Enriched with
bold baroque scrolls and acanthus leafage. With original polychromy.

Height, 29 inches

[304]

304 FINELY CARVED WALNUT CENTRE TABLE

SPANISH, 17TH CENTURY

A sturdily built table equipped with three drawers on one side. Richly carved with large rosettes and scroll medallions in low relief in shaped panels. The borders with bands of conventionalized acanthus leaves; slightly overlapping massive top. Ring-turned supports with square stretchers. Fine patina.

Height, 33 inches; length, 7 feet 5½ inches; width, 29 inches

[SEE ILLUSTRATION]

85

305 **WALNUT AND PINE TABOURET WITH ONE DRAWER**

SPANISH, EARLY 18TH CENTURY

With scroll and trellis carved front. On moulded and slightly raked end supports with stretchers. *Height, 18 inches; width, 26 inches*

306 **PAIR OF WROUGHT IRON ANDIRONS** SPANISH, CIRCA 1700

The tall pillars capped by ball finials and with twisted brackets with floriated tops; on splayed supports. (2) *Height, 29 inches*

307 **PAIR OF WROUGHT IRON ANDIRONS** SPANISH, 18TH CENTURY

With tapered baluster pillars embellished with leaf motifs, ball finials; splayed bases. (2) *Height, 25 inches*

308 **PAIR OF WROUGHT IRON ANDIRONS** SPANISH, 18TH CENTURY

With twisted pillars, ball finials and splayed bases. (2)

Height, 17½ inches

309 **CARVED AND GILDED BAROQUE MIRROR**

SPANISH, LATE 17TH CENTURY

The rectangular frame richly carved in high relief with scroll acanthus and open shells. *Height, 26 inches; width, 22 inches*

310 **SMALL WALNUT SIDE TABLE WITH ONE DRAWER**

SPANISH, EARLY 17TH CENTURY

The front carved with acanthus medallions in rectangular panels. On ball-turned supports with plain stretchers. Dark patina.

Height, 28 inches; width, 31 inches

311 **WALNUT ARMCHAIR** SPANISH, 17TH CENTURY

The back and the seat frame handsomely pierced and carved with bold scroll and acanthus motifs. Straight arms, supports and panelled seat.

86

[312]

312 ARMS OF A BISHOP IN PAINTED AND SCULPTURED STONE

SPANISH, 16TH CENTURY

In four sections. Displaying an upright quartered shield charged with two lions, two crescents, miniature castles, and "Ave Maria," surrounded by rich scrolls and sprays of acanthus leafage. Limestone, carved in high relief, painted and gilded.

From a house in the province of Leon.

Height, 52 inches; width, 44 inches

[SEE ILLUSTRATION]

87

313 **VELVET-COVERED VESTMENT CHEST** SPANISH, 17TH CENTURY
Rectangular, with slightly domed lid. Covered in contemporary crimson velvet stamped with all-over design of fleurettes and with handsome gold galloons. Has two fine pierced circular iron locks, corner mounts and side handles showing traces of gilding.
From a private collection in Madrid.

Height, 21 inches; length, 49 inches; width, 24 inches

314 **SMALL WALNUT AND PINE TABOURET**

SPANISH, 17TH CENTURY
Rectangular top, on splayed trestle supports.

Height, 16 inches; width, 20 inches

315 **CARVED SMALL WALNUT SIDE TABLE**

SPANISH, 17TH CENTURY
Unusually fine ball and collar turned supports with plain stretchers; ball feet restored. Apron, stiles and two drawers with elaborate geometrical carving in low relief. Dark patina.
From Estremadura.

Size of top, 39 x 24 inches

316 **THREE SMALL WALNUT CHAIRS** SPANISH, 17TH CENTURY
Two with rectangular backs, plain seats, ring-turned supports and plain stretchers. One with arcaded back, containing ring-turned spindles. Similar spindles below the seat. (3)

ONE OF A PAIR OF PANELLED
WALNUT SACRISTY DOORS
SPANISH, SEVENTEENTH CENTURY

[317]

317 PAIR OF PANELLED WALNUT SACRISTY DOORS

SPANISH, 17TH CENTURY

In splendid condition, with rich reddish-brown patina and retaining the original iron handles, shell-shaped latches, hinges and locks. Each door is panelled with raised mouldings, forming a rich geometrical design with cruciform centres.

From the monastery of Paula, near Madrid. (2)

Height, 5 feet 11 inches; width, 3 feet 3 inches

[SEE ILLUSTRATION]

318 **TWO BRASS CANDLESTICKS**   SPANISH, EARLY 18TH CENTURY
With wide circular bases and baluster stems. (2)

Height, 9¼ inches

319 **CARVED AND GILDED LOUIS XVI TRUMEAU MIRROR**
Mounted above the mirror glass with a painted canvas panel depicting a fête champêtre, with Boucher figures of children standing in a cornfield. Gilded frame carved with ribbon twist motif.

Height, 6 feet 2 inches; width, 34 inches

320 **PAINTED AND CARVED ARMCHAIR OF THE REGENCE PERIOD**   FRENCH, EARLY 18TH CENTURY
The shaped back, seat and armrests covered in flowered bright blue silk brocade. Walnut frame carved with shell and scroll ornaments, painted and gilded. Gracefully voluted arms and cabriole legs.

321 **SMALL WALNUT GATELEG TABLE**
SPANISH, EARLY 17TH CENTURY
Circular top, supported by four vase and ring turned legs and two pivoted gates, with plain stretchers.   *Diameter of top, 33 inches*

90

ONE OF A PAIR OF WALNUT
MARQUETRY SIDE CHAIRS
DUTCH, EARLY EIGHTEENTH CENTURY

[322]

322 PAIR OF WALNUT MARQUETRY SIDE CHAIRS

DUTCH, EARLY 18TH CENTURY

Charming pair in the Queen Anne taste. The shaped high backs centred with vase-shaped splats. Crest elaborately carved with shells and foliage scrolls. Shell-carved cabriole supports with eagle claw and ball feet; curved stretchers. Seats covered in crimson silk brocatelle. (2)

[SEE ILLUSTRATION]

323 **PAINTED AND PANELLED DOOR**   VENETIAN, 18TH CENTURY
Occupied by four sunken panels with raised mouldings, each painted
with allegorical female figures seated under domed canopies. Pairs
of winged amorini below. Painted blue with yellow borders.

Height, 6 feet 2 inches; width, 4 feet 1 inch

324 **PAIR OF PANELLED WALNUT SHUTTERS**

SPANISH, EARLY 17TH CENTURY
The centres embellished with star-shaped mouldings framed by
grooved stiles. Retaining the original wrought iron lock, latch and
hasp. (2)   *Size of each, 38 x 23½ inches*

325 **PAIR OF CARVED AND GILDED LANTERN TORCHERES**

SPANISH, EARLY 18TH CENTURY
A highly decorated pair of vestibule or porch lanterns. Hexagonal,
with dome top and handsome carving of acanthus scrolls and bird
forms framing the shaped glass panels. Mounted on damask-covered
modern standards with moulded square bases. Fitted for electricity. (2)   *Height, 8 feet 8 inches*

326 **PAIR OF BRASS ALTAR CANDLESTICKS**

SPANISH, 18TH CENTURY
With baluster stems, wide circular bobèches and bases. Inscribed
under the bases, "Ca. Ds. Jns.," presumably the name of the church
from which they came. (2)   *Height, 7½ inches*

[327]

327 VERY FINE CARVED WALNUT CENTRE TABLE

SPANISH, LATE 16TH CENTURY

Panelled on one side and fitted on the opposite side with four drawers. Ornamented with bands of thumb carving framing oval and square carved medallions. Each drawer has two wrought iron drop handles and diamond-shaped keyplates. Stands on six sturdy vase-turned supports with heavy stretchers.

Purchased from a collection in Pamplona.

Height, 30 inches; length, 10 feet 6 inches; width, 28 inches

[SEE ILLUSTRATION]

328 WALNUT AND VELVET ARMCHAIR

SPANISH, EARLY 17TH CENTURY

The low back and broad seat covered in contemporary crimson silk velvet with red and gold fringe. Plain square supports, shaped arms and front stretcher.

329 SMALL CABINET SECRETAIRE

NORTHERN ITALIAN, 17TH CENTURY

Fitted with eight small drawers with moulded fronts. The fall front, top and sides, incised with Renaissance allegorical figures flanking armorial cartouche; moulded borders.

Height, 18½ inches; width, 25 inches

330 WALNUT CENTRE TABLE ON SCROLLED SUPPORTS

SPANISH, 17TH CENTURY

Medium size, and probably the handsomest one in the collection. The top is plain and slightly overlaps the supports, which are lyre shape, magnificently carved with various floral forms and pendent husk swags, boldly scrolled and braced by leaf-enriched, curved iron stretchers. *Length, 4 feet 4 inches; width, 30 inches*

331 PAIR OF CARVED PINE CONVENT DOORS

SPANISH, 16TH CENTURY

The lower part carved in relief with the crowned double eagle, imperial insignia of Charles V. The upper parts have hinged doors carved with symbols of the Host. Framed by raised borders. Some restoration. (2)   *Height, 6 feet 8 inches; width, 2 feet 5 inches*

94

CARVED AND POLYCHROME WOOD FIGURES

[332]

332 CARVED AND POLYCHROME FIGURE OF A DONOR

SPANISH, 15TH CENTURY

Standing figure of a man of rank wearing the short tunic with bulbous sleeves and the tight hose of the period. His cloak is draped loosely about his shoulders. In his left hand he holds a Gothic chalice. The full features are expressively carved and framed by thick folds of curled hair, which fall to the shoulders. The figure stands upon a moulded and flaring plinth. Red, blue and gold polychromy.

From the monastery of Burgo de Osma, in the province of Soria.

Height, 39 inches

333 SMALL CARVED AND GILDED RELIEF PANEL

SPANISH, 16TH CENTURY

Representing a standing figure of a saint holding a book of the Gospels.　　　*Height, 13 inches; width, 6½ inches*

[334]

334 **CARVED AND POLYCHROME WOOD FIGURE OF SANTA
BARBARA**   SPANISH, LATE 15TH CENTURY
Standing figure, her hands clasped in an attitude of prayer (one
hand missing). Her robes painted a rich, deep blue and dotted with
gold stars. Her hair hangs in deep folds around the sides of the
head and down the back. At her feet are carved three angels' heads.
A very fine example of early Spanish wood carving showing strong
French influence.
From a convent in Laquetio.   *Height, 36½ inches*

[SEE ILLUSTRATION]

335 **CARVED AND POLYCHROME WOOD STATUE**
                                         SPANISH, 17TH CENTURY
Standing figure of St. Maximono wearing richly gilded and painted
chasuble and mitre. His right hand held in the attitude of blessing.
Standing on a shaped wood plinth inscribed with the Saint's name.
                                Height with plinth, 28½ inches

96

336 CARVED AND POLYCHROME WOOD STATUE

SPANISH, 17TH CENTURY

Standing figure of Santa Lucia holding the emblem of her martyrdom. Her draperies finely carved in graceful folds, gilded and polychromed. Standing on a pentagonal plinth which bears the Saint's name. *Height with plinth, 27½ inches*

337 PAINTED AND CARVED ARMORIAL PLAQUE

SPANISH, 17TH CENTURY

A circular cartouche of pierced, carved and gilded acanthus scrolls containing a painted armorial shield. Mounted on crimson damask-covered backboard. *Diameter, 26 inches*

338 THREE CARVED AND GILDED WOOD STATUETTES OF
SAINTS SPANISH, 18TH CENTURY

Charming small standing figures of St. Matthew, St. Mark and St. John, with their emblems. On moulded circular plinths enriched with bands of floral arabesques. (3)

From the collection of Jose A. Brussi, Barcelona.

Height, 17 inches

OBJECTS IN BRONZE

NUMBERS 339-344

339 TWO SMALL BRONZE TAPER STICKS SPANISH, CIRCA 1700

With pierced sconces and moulded circular bases. (2)

Height, 4 inches

340 TWO BRONZE LION FINIALS SPANISH, 16TH CENTURY

Gothic lion heads of archaic form. One with petalled base, the other with pierced base. Rare. (2) *Height, 4 inches*

341 SMALL BRONZE BELL FLEMISH, 16TH CENTURY

Decorated with portrait medallions in floral wreaths depending from festoons. Handle formed of three sprays of acanthus leaves. Piece missing from rim. *Height, 4½ inches*

[342]

342 **IMPORTANT GOTHIC BRONZE MORTAR**   SPANISH, CIRCA 1500
With wide flaring rim and open side handles. Decorated in relief
with representations of the Madonna and Child standing under
Gothic tracery arches. The rim encircled by an inscription in Latin.
Height, 14 inches; diameter, 18 inches

[SEE ILLUSTRATION]

343 **BRONZE MORTAR**   SPANISH, ·16TH CENTURY
The flaring moulded rim with rope-twist border. The sides deco-
rated with narrow pilasters and urns of flowers.
Height, 4¼ inches; diameter, 5½ inches

344 **BRONZE MORTAR**   SPANISH, 16TH CENTURY
Of nearly similar shape to the preceding, with open side handles.
From the Sir John Laking Collection.
Height, 4 inches; diameter, 5½ inches

98

345 **LONG WALNUT SIDE TABLE WITH FOUR DRAWERS**

SPANISH, 17TH CENTURY

For use as a side or centre table. Standing on bold lyre-shaped end supports and with four small drawers at one side of the deeply moulded frame. Each drawer finely carved in low relief with quatrefoil and scrolled leaf motifs. Iron drop handles and shaped keyplates. *Length, 6 feet 6 inches; width, 32 inches*

346 **FOUR WALNUT SPINDLE-BACK SIDE CHAIRS**

SPANISH, 17TH CENTURY

With open arcaded backs in two tiers, scroll crests and turned finials. Panelled seats; turned supports and stretchers. (4)

347 **PAIR OF WROUGHT IRON ANDIRONS** SPANISH, 18TH CENTURY

With handsomely scrolled pillars and bases. Ball finials. (2)

Height, 21 inches

348 **PAIR OF WROUGHT IRON ANDIRONS** SPANISH, 18TH CENTURY

Nearly similar to the preceding, but smaller. (2)

Height, 15½ inches

349 **PAIR OF ANDIRONS** SPANISH, CIRCA 1700

Handsome pair, with partly twisted and tapered iron pillars with small guard brackets and small brass finials. Boldly splayed bases. (2) *Height about 28 inches*

350 **TURNED WALNUT SMALL BENCH COVERED IN SILK BROCADE** SPANISH, 17TH CENTURY

With slightly tapered and turned supports; vase and ring turned stretchers. The top covered in antique flowered silk brocade with deep braided and tasselled fringe.

Height, 15 inches; width, 24 inches

99

351 RARE CARVED WALNUT VARGUENO ON CHEST STAND

SPANISH, 16TH CENTURY

Rectangular body enclosed by a let-down front with handsome decoration of arabesque medallions in gilded and pierced iron, backed by
crimson velvet. Interior fitted with numerous small drawers and
lockers, simulating miniature porticos or tabernacles of spiral
twisted columns partly gilded and enriched with a mosaic design of
small painted bone insets. Has the original Moorish pattern iron
lock and wrought handles. Stands on a chest base, equipped with
four drawers with diamond-shaped mouldings, each centred by iron
crowned cartouches upon oval medallions, serving as the key escutcheons. Shell-carved draw-bars support the fall-front.
From a private house in Salamanca.

Height, 56 *inches; width*, 41 *inches*

[SEE ILLUSTRATION]

352 PAIR OF TALL BRASS CANDLESTICKS FRENCH, 17TH CENTURY
With foliated pricket tops, slightly tapered baluster stems and
scrolled triangular baroque bases. Rare. (2) *Height*, 25½ *inches*

353 MANTEL CLOCK IN RED LACQUER CASE BY JAMES SMITH,
LONDON   CIRCA 1730
Arched brass dial with silvered hour ring and subsidiary dial and
with very fine gilded and chased metal arabesque mounts. Striking
the hours and half hours. Eight-day run. In domed case, gilded
with Chinese figures on red lacquer ground. (As is)

Height, 20 *inches; width*, 11 *inches*

354 GOTHIC PAINTED AND GILDED GESSO RELIQUARY BOX

SPANISH, 15TH CENTURY

Of walnut, coated with gesso and painted in colors and gold with
figures of saints in seven circular medallions surrounded by raised
arabesque flowers and borders of inscriptions. Rectangular, with
slightly domed lid; wrought iron hinges and bronze hasp. Rare.
From a convent near Logrono.

Height, 4½ *inches; width*, 9 *inches*

100

RARE CARVED WALNUT VARGUENO
ON CHEST STAND
SPANISH, SIXTEENTH CENTURY

[351]

355 **IMPORTANT LOUIS XV WALNUT AND NEEDLEWORK**
    ARMCHAIR   FRENCH, CIRCA 1750
    A splendidly proportioned chair. The wide shaped needlework
    back designed with Ohpheus holding a lyre and seated on the bank
    of a stream, buildings to the right. The wide and slightly curved
    needlework seat shows exotic birds and flowers in rich colors upon
    a dark ground. The voluted and grooved arms also in needlework.
    On slender cabriole supports with scroll feet.
    Purchased from M. Harris, London.

[SEE ILLUSTRATION]

356 **MAHOGANY BUREAU A CYLINDRE OF THE LOUIS XVI**
    PERIOD   FRENCH, 18TH CENTURY
    With small drawers, compartments and leather-lined writing slide
    enclosed by a cylinder shutter; also small drawers above and below.
    Top with brass gallery. Stands on tapered and fluted legs.
    Height, 3 feet 11 inches; width, 4 feet 6 inches

357 **TURNED WALNUT ARMCHAIR**   SPANISH, 17TH CENTURY
    In the Louis XIII style. The slightly canted rectangular back and
    seat covered in rose-figured pink silk fabric. Curved and scrolled
    arms, turned supports and stretchers.

IMPORTANT LOUIS QUINZE WALNUT
AND NEEDLEWORK ARMCHAIR
FRENCH, CIRCA 1750

[355]

358 ARAGONESE EXTENSION CENTRE TABLE

SPANISH, CIRCA 1600

A dining table of very fine proportions constructed of solid walnut
with brown patina. The under structure consisting of end pedestals.
formed as S scrolls enriched with carved rosaces and standing on leaf
carved and tapered shoes. A balustraded medial stretcher runs the
length of the table and has three ball-turned uprights. At the corners are pendent baluster finials. Under leaves at either end can
be drawn out.

Length, 5 feet 8 inches; width, 31 inches; width of extension leaves,

31 inches

[SEE ILLUSTRATION]

359 **VERY FINE SILVER LARGE TAZZA**   SPANISH, CIRCA 1700-1710
Chased and engraved with a large rosace from which radiate exceptionally fine palmettes of birds and floral arabesques, each differing
in some special motif. The border is delicately reeded. On baluster
socle and flaring circular foot with similar floral decoration.

Height, 5 inches; diameter, 12½ inches

[SEE ILLUSTRATION]

[360]   [359]   [360]

[358]

360 PAIR OF LOUIS XVI SILVER CANDELABRA

FRENCH, CIRCA 1780-90

A most desirable pair in the chaste Classic style of the period. The stems, slightly tapered and fluted, have wide circular bases and urn tops from which radiate three reeded and curved branches bearing urn sconces. The circular bobèches have delicately pierced trellised galleries. The borders finely chiselled with bandeaux of husk ornament and beading. Paris mark. (2)   *Height,* 16½ *inches*

[SEE ILLUSTRATION]

361 **SET OF FOUR SILVER SHAPED TRENCHER SALTCELLARS**
ITALIAN, EARLY 18TH CENTURY
In the Louis XV style. Of handsome scroll form with oval balls.
Engraved with a small crest and motto "Fides sufficit". Rare. (4)
Width, 4¼ inches

362 **OVAL SILVER CONDIMENT BOX**   SPANISH, 18TH CENTURY
With double hinged lid, beaded borders and compartmented interior.
Finely engraved with a coat-of-arms and floral arabesques. Stands
on four ball feet. Maker's mark under the base.   *Width, 4½ inches*

363 **OVAL SILVER CONDIMENT BOX**   SPANISH, DATED 1711
With double hinged lid, reeded borders and four claw and ball feet.
Engraved with letters "F.A." Rare.   *Width, 4 inches*

364 **TURNED WALNUT ARMCHAIR**   SPANISH, 17TH CENTURY
The slender gently curved arms terminating in scrolls. Baluster-
turned supports and stretchers. The rectangular back and seat
covered in rose-figured green silk.

365 **OPEN VARGUENO ON TURNED STAND**
SPANISH, EARLY 17TH CENTURY
Containing seven small drawers and a centre door exposing three
drawers. Richly carved and gilded and inlaid with bone. Pierced
iron corner mounts and side handles. On table stand with finely
turned and slightly raked supports braced by plain stretchers.
Height, 4 feet 5 inches; width, 3 feet 7 inches

366 **SMALL WALNUT SIDE TABLE WITH TWO DRAWERS**
SPANISH; 17TH CENTURY
The oblong top slightly overlaps the frame, which is shaped in the
front and contains two rosette-carved drawers. Vase and collar
turned supports with plain stretchers.   *Size of top, 37 x 23 inches*

367 **PAIR OF SMALL PANELLED AND CARVED DOORS**
SPANISH, 17TH CENTURY
Each occupied by large and small rectangular panels chamferred and
moulded and framed by carved stiles. Pleasing pair. (2)
Size of each, 56 x 25 inches

ONE OF A SET OF EIGHT
WALNUT AND NEEDLEWORK CHAIRS
SPANISH, SEVENTEENTH CENTURY

[368]

368 SET OF EIGHT VERY FINE WALNUT AND NEEDLEWORK
     CHAIRS   SPANISH, 17TH CENTURY
     The rectangular backs and seats covered in antique silk needlework,
     designed with baroque flowers and foliage in colors. The supports
     and stretchers finely turned in ball pattern. A most desirable and
     very rare set of neddlework chairs, showing French influence. (8)

              [SEE ILLUSTRATION]

369 **POLYCHROMED AND WROUGHT TIN CHURCH LANTERN**

SPANISH, 17TH CENTURY

Octagonal, with tapered base and domed top, surmounted by cruciform motifs. Richly pierced in a trellis pattern and ornamented with scrolled acanthus leaves. Similar to the lanterns in the Church of St. Jose, Madrid. *Height, 47 inches*

370 **PAINTED AND CARVED BEDSTEAD IN THE CHINESE TASTE**

SPANISH, 18TH CENTURY

The shaped high headboard painted and gilded with Chinese buildings and foliage on a dark green ground and outlined by carved rocaille scrolls, stalactite and pendent flower ornament. Has four low carved posts. *Width, 4 feet 8 inches*

371 **TURNED WALNUT ARMCHAIR** SPANISH, 17TH CENTURY

With handsome spirally turned supports and stretchers, and gently curved and scrolled arms; the rectangular back and seat covered in red and yellow brocatelle with silk fringe.

372 **DECORATED RED LACQUER CABINET SECRETARY WITH BOMBE BASE** VENETIAN, EARLY 18TH CENTURY

In the Régence taste. Decorated with panels of Chinese figures, birds and trees slightly raised and gilded upon a ground of rich red lacquer. The upper part is crested by a handsome scrolled pediment with five ball and spike finials and has an arched and moulded door enclosing compartments and small drawers. A slant writing flap at the centre encloses small drawers. The bombé shaped base contains a large drawer. The piece stands on short cabriole supports with "Spanish" feet. *Height, 7 feet 4 inches; width, 3 feet*

[SEE ILLUSTRATION]

108

DECORATED RED LACQUER
CABINET SECRETARY
VENETIAN, EARLY EIGHTEENTH CENTURY

[372]

373 MARINE PAINTING ATTRIBUTED TO PETER MONAMY

ENGLISH, EARLY 18TH CENTURY

Depicting a naval engagement between English and Dutch men-of-war. In the foreground are two vessels engaged in heavy bombardment. Other vessels in the distance are in flames. Painted in strong colors, the choppy water a shadowy gray. The sky is filled with storm clouds shading from a soft pink to a deep black. On canvas. Carved and gilded frame. *Size, 37 x 60 inches*

374 FLOWER PAINTING ON PANEL BY BENITO ESPINOS

SPANISH, CIRCA 1787

Depicting a classic urn of summer flowers finely painted in colors upon a dark background. The urn stands upon a marble slab. Signed "Benito Espinos Fecit" at the lower left. On cradled panel. Leaf-carved and gilded frame. *Size, 34½ x 22¼ inches*

Benito Espinos, born in Valencia, was the son of Joseph Espinos, and in 1787 was made director of the Royal Academy of San Carlos at Valencia. He died in 1817. Works by him are in the Madrid Gallery, Museum of Valencia, and the Escorial Palace.

375 DECORATED SEMICIRCULAR CONSOLE TABLE

ENGLISH, 18TH CENTURY

The top and rounded apron decorated with festoons of flowers, shells and butterflies in medallions painted and engraved on paper and applied to the wood. On tapered square supports. One leg damaged. *Width, 42½ inches*

376 CARVED AND GILDED SMALL MIRROR

SPANISH, 17TH CENTURY

The square frame richly carved with large acanthus leaves and shell motifs in high relief. *Size, 23 x 20 inches*

377 **PAIR OF BRASS CANDLESTICKS** SPANISH, EARLY 18TH CENTURY
With tapered baluster stems and wide circular bases. (2)
Height, 8¾ inches

378 **WALNUT SIDE TABLE WITH TWO DRAWERS**
SPANISH, 17TH CENTURY
The deep frame bordered by a deep flaring moulding, elaborately
carved. The two drawers at one side carved with eccentric diamond-
shaped medallions in low relief. On ring-turned supports; plain
stretchers. Brown patina.   *Length, 6 feet; width, 26½ inches*

379 **CARVED AND POLYCHROME RELIQUARY BOX**
SPANISH, EARLY 17TH CENTURY
Small rectangular box with hinged lid and wrought iron lock and
handles. Covered with gesso, decorated with raised grotesque and
arabesque foliage, partly gilded.
From a private collection in Madrid.   *Size, 15 x 11½ inches*

380 **CARVED WALNUT AND VELVET BENCH**
SPANISH, LATE 17TH CENTURY
Boldly scrolled supports braced by similarly scrolled medial stretcher.
Top covered in ruby silk velvet with gold galloon. *Width, 28 inches*

381 **OVAL WALNUT GATELEG TABLE**   SPANISH, 17TH CENTURY
A centre or dining table with a drawer at either end, below which
the frame is gracefully shaped and carved with floral sprays and
open shells. Supported by finely turned legs and a pair of pivoted
gates. Plain square stretchers.   *Size of top, 60 x 50 inches*

111

TWO IMPORTANT PAINTED WOOD CEILINGS FROM A FIFTEENTH

CENTURY HOUSE IN FRIBOURG, SWITZERLAND

ATTRIBUTED TO CHARLES LEBRUN

NUMBERS 382-383

382 IMPORTANT PAINTED WOOD CEILING ATTRIBUTED TO
CHARLES LEBRUN   FRENCH, LATE 17TH CENTURY
The centre painted to represent the sky, shows an allegorical female
figure floating among clouds, blowing a horn and holding the palm
of Victory. At the four corners are groups of genii supporting
armorial cartouches which bear crowned royal insignia. These
figures hold in their hands flower festoons which depend from beautiful scroll cartouches on two sides; the two remaining sides are
occupied by blue and white Rouen jardinières of flowers which stand
upon parapets under acanthus-enriched architraves.

Approximate size, 16 feet x 11 feet 6 inches

Charles Lebrun is known to have executed work of this kind for his
various patrons, and the fine drawing and coloring seen in these two
ceilings lead one to accept the attribution made for them.

[SEE ILLUSTRATION]

112

PAINTED WOOD CEILING
ATTRIBUTED TO CHARLES LEBRUN
FRENCH, SEVENTEENTH CENTURY

[382]

FIFTEENTH CENTURY HOUSE
IN FRIBOURG, SWITZERLAND
FROM WHICH WERE TAKEN THE
PAINTED WOOD CEILINGS
ATTRIBUTED TO CHARLES LEBRUN

[NUMBERS 382 AND 383]

383 **IMPORTANT PAINTED WOOD CEILING ATTRIBUTED TO
CHARLES LEBRUN**   FRENCH, LATE 17TH CENTURY
Of similar design to the preceding; the centre occupied by a draped
figure of Venus and group of amorini floating among clouds. Some
of the panels were slightly damaged by fire but have been effectively
restored.   *Approximate size, 16 feet* x 11 *feet 6 inches*

[SEE ILLUSTRATION]

114

PAINTED WOOD CEILING
ATTRIBUTED TO CHARLES LEBRUN
FRENCH, SEVENTEENTH CENTURY

[383]

384 PAIR OF TURNED WALNUT AND VELVET ARMCHAIRS

SPANISH, 17TH CENTURY

The straight arms, front legs and stretchers finely turned in ball and ring pattern. The low rectangular backs and seats covered in blue velvet with gold galloons of later date. (2)

385 LONG WALNUT BENCH   SPANISH, 17TH CENTURY

Wainscot seat with simple lines. Hinged and panelled back. Splayed trestle end supports with wrought iron brace.

Length, 6 feet 7 inches

386 RICHLY CARVED WALNUT CENTRE TABLE

SPANISH, EARLY 17TH CENTURY

With two drawers on side. Carved all around with very fine circular and oblong acanthus-leaf medallions. The drawer fronts with panels of foliage arabesques. On vase and ring turned sturdy supports braced by moulded side and medial stretchers. Fine light brown patina.

From Soria.   *Length, 5 feet 1 inch; width, 30 inches*

387 PAIR OF WROUGHT IRON ANDIRONS   SPANISH, 18TH CENTURY

Pleasing pair, with shaped pillars and splayed bases. (2)

Height, 26 inches

388 PAIR OF WROUGHT IRON ANDIRONS   SPANISH, 18TH CENTURY

Nearly similar to the preceding, but smaller. (2)

Height, 21 inches

[389]

389 IMPORTANT SIX-FOLD PAINTED LEATHER SCREEN

FRENCH, 18TH CENTURY

Each panel is occupied by male and female figures in Persian cos-
tumes, painted on a silver-gray ground. These exotic figures standing on shaped dais enriched with satyr-masks, are framed with a
magnificiently scrolled border, entwined among which are grotesque
animal forms, flowers and mascarons in heavy leaf gilding and
tooled work.

This exceedingly charming French screen in the Persian taste was
obtained from the private collection of a former French ambassador
residing near Bordeaux.

Size per panel, 5 feet 10 inches x 23 inches

[SEE ILLUSTRATION]

117

390 PAIR OF CARVED WALNUT AND VELVET BAROQUE
ARMCHAIRS   SPANISH OR PORTUGUESE, CIRCA 1700
The finely proportioned high backs and seats covered in emerald-
green velvet with gold galloons. Voluted arms richly carved with
sprays of honeysuckle and large acanthus motifs. On square cabriole supports braced by curved stretchers also richly carved. (2)

391 WALNUT WITHDRAWING TABLE WITH SPLAYED SUPPORTS
                              SPANISH, 17TH CENTURY
Heavy rectangular top with two draw-out extension leaves at either
end, with spool-turned and raked end supports with similarly turned
stretchers and curved iron strengthening brace. Dark patina. Leaves
restored.
Length, 51 inches, extending to 7 feet 7 inches; width, 29 inches

SPANISH IRON REJA, ETC.

NUMBERS 392-404

392 TWO GILDED IRON APPLIQUES   SPANISH, 17TH CENTURY
Foliated candle branches with pierced and scalloped circular
bobèches. Rare. (2)   *Length, 9 inches*

393 IRON GRILL   SPANISH, 18TH CENTURY
With slender bars in geometrical formation, embellished with circular rosettes.   *Size, 5 feet 2 inches x 4 feet 7 inches*

394 PAIR OF WROUGHT IRON GOTHIC CANDLESTICKS
                              SPANISH, 15TH CENTURY
Extremely interesting pair, of handsome design. With circular
tray bases and tripod quatrefoil feet. Pricket tops. Almost identi-
cal with a pair illustrated in the catalogue by Galdacano of "Exposicion de Hierros Antiquos Españoles". (2)   *Height, 16 inches*

395 PAIR OF WROUGHT IRON TRIPOD TORCHERES
                              SPANISH, 17TH CENTURY
With wide circular bobèches for pricket candle lights. Standing
on tripod supports. Rare. (2)   *Height, 46 inches*

118

[396]

396 **BRASS CHANDELIER**   SPANISH, CIRCA 1700
Hanging light fixtures in two tiers with eight scroll branches radiating from a centre baluster hub. Wide circular bobèches.
From a church in the province of Lerida.   *Height, 24 inches*

[SEE ILLUSTRATION]

397 **WROUGHT IRON LARGE BALCONY**
                            SPANISH, EARLY 18TH CENTURY
Pleasing design of two tiers of slender cluster colonnades with fleuretted tops. At each end are brass ball finials. Retains the old light-colored paint.
   Height, 3 feet 3 inches; length, 9 feet 2 inches; depth, 28 inches

398 **WROUGHT IRON GRILL**   SPANISH, EARLY 18TH CENTURY
Of similar design to the preceding balcony.
            Height, 6 feet 10 inches; width, 4 feet 6 inches

399 **CHISELLED STEEL BIT**   SPANISH, 16TH CENTURY
Double bar bit with wide strap rings. Finely chiselled, the rings inlaid with gold. Rare.   *Width, 9 inches*

119

400 **IRON LOCK, HASP AND KEY**   SPANISH, 17TH CENTURY
Of cartouche form, finely pierced; original hasp.

Width, 11½ *inches*

401 **SMALL IRON GRILL**   SPANISH, 17TH CENTURY
From a convent door. In a trellis design with arched top.

Size about 20 x 11 *inches*

[402]

402 **IRON GRILL**   SPANISH, 16TH CENTURY
Charming design of flower motifs and rosettes interlaced with vertical balusters forming a pleasing Gothic pattern. Rare.

Height, 4 *feet* 7 *inches; length,* 4 *feet* 3 *inches; depth,* 10 *inches*

[SEE ILLUSTRATION]

120

NEEDLEWORK AND TEXTILES, INCLUDING

AN IMPORTANT SPANISH CARPET

403 **LONG STRIP OF RUBY-RED VELVET**   SPANISH, 17TH CENTURY

Rich deep color and condition; with braided borders.
Length, 13 *feet; width,* 21 *inches*

404 **LONG STRIP OF RUBY-RED VELVET**   SPANISH, 17TH CENTURY
Similar to the preceding.   *Length,* 13 *feet; width,* 21 *inches*

405 **LONG STRIP OF RUBY-RED VELVET**   SPANISH, 17TH CENTURY
Similar to the preceding.   *Length,* 13 *feet; width,* 21 *inches*

406 **TWO PANELS OF FIGURED CRIMSON SILK DAMASK**
SPANISH, EARLY 18TH CENTURY
Patterned with medallions of bold flowers and leaves in two shades
of red. Comprising four strips each 3 yards long.
Total length about 12 *yards*

407 **SILVER AND SILK BROCADE ALTAR FRONTAL**
SPANISH, 18TH CENTURY
Designed with scrolled flower and leaf forms in silver thread and
red silk upon a pink ground. Panelled with silver galloons.
Size, 7 *feet* 8 *inches* x 3 *feet*

408 **FIGURED CRIMSON SILK DAMASK HANGING**
SPANISH, 18TH CENTURY
Patterned with boldly scrolled leaves and flowers and trimmed with
silk fringe on three sides. Composed of four strips of two and one-
half yards. Linen lined.   *Totalling about* 10 *yards*

[409 AND 410]

409 **IMPORTANT RENAISSANCE PETIT-POINT NEEDLEWORK PANEL**   FRENCH, 16TH CENTURY

Illustrating four scenes from the story of Adam and Eve, beginning with the temptation in the Garden, secondly the expulsion from the Garden by the angel; the remaining two scenes depict Adam and Eve working at cultivating the soil. Dividing the various subjects are seated allegorical female figures of heroic size. Bordered in braided silk and wool and mounted on pine stretchers.

Length, 8 feet 3 inches; width, 16 inches

From the collection of Baron Marochetti, Château de Vaux sur Seine, near St. Germain en Laye.

[SEE ILLUSTRATION]

410 **IMPORTANT RENAISSANCE PETIT-POINT NEEDLEWORK PANEL**   FRENCH, 16TH CENTURY

The companion panel to the preceding, depicting what is presumed to be the representation of the return of the Prodigal Son. At the right a youth is advancing toward an elderly figure, behind whom stand numerous male and female figures in rich attire. At the extreme right peasants are seen approaching carrying baskets of fruits. Both this and the preceding panel have exceptionally fine landscape background somewhat in the Breughel style, showing various types of architectural buildings and foliage. The perspective in one panel is unusually fine.   *Length, 8 feet 3 inches; width, 16 inches*

From the collection of Baron Marochetti, Château de Vaux sur Seine, near St. Germain en Laye.

[SEE ILLUSTRATION]

411 CRIMSON SILK DAMASK BEDSPREAD

SPANISH, EARLY 18TH CENTURY

Patterned with bold flower and leaf medallions. Comprising four strips, each three yards long. Bordered with yellow fringe.

Totalling about 12 1/3 yards

412 PANEL OF FIGURED CRIMSON SILK DAMASK

SPANISH, EARLY 18TH CENTURY

Similar to the preceding. Composed of six strips cut at the edges.

Total length about 14 yards

413 PANEL OF FIGURED CRIMSON SILK DAMASK

SPANISH, 18TH CENTURY

Of similar design to the preceding. Composed of four strips, each two and three-quarter yards long. *Totalling about 11 yards*

414 PANEL OF FIGURED CRIMSON SILK DAMASK

SPANISH, 18TH CENTURY

Of similar design to the preceding. Composed of five strips, each two and one-half yards long. *Total length about 12 yards*

415 EMBROIDERED RED VELVET CAPE   SPANISH, 18TH CENTURY

A rich ruby velvet. The border finely embroidered with meandered floral vines in gold thread and sequins. *Width about 50 inches*

416 CRIMSON SILK DAMASK PANEL   SPANISH, 18TH CENTURY

Medium design, formal flowers and leaves in two shades of brilliant red. *Size about 7 feet x 8 feet*

417 RED SILK DAMASK PANEL   SPANISH, 18TH CENTURY

With large leaf and flower design in two shades of crimson.

Size about 7 feet square

418 RED SILK DAMASK PANEL   SPANISH, 18TH CENTURY

Similar to the preceding.   *Size about 8 feet x 9 feet*

123

419 YELLOW SILK DAMASK BEDSPREAD
SPANISH, EARLY 18TH CENTURY
With bold appliquéd flower and scroll medallion design in white silk
on a flowered yellow ground. Linen lined. *Size about 8 feet x 7 feet*

420 BLUE SILK BROCADE BEDSPREAD   SPANISH, 18TH CENTURY
Pleasing design of small flower posies in rich colors on pale blue
ground. Linen lined.   *Size, 6 feet square*

421 PANEL OF RED SILK BROCADE   SPANISH, 18TH CENTURY
Displaying sprays of slightly conventionalized roses and leaves in
bright colored silks on a red ground.
Size, 5 feet 7 inches x 4 feet 9 inches

422 IMPORTANT SPANISH WOOLEN CARPET EARLY 18TH CENTURY
The rich blue field is centred by a coat-of-arms, around which are
grouped human figures and detached flower forms, the remainder
of the field being occupied by two very fine floral cartouches somewhat in the baroque taste. This design is executed in bright shades
of orange-yellow, turquoise-blue, green and two shades of rose-red,
which are in striking contrast to the deeper tone of the background.
The three borders show medallions and urns of flowers and conventional flower vines, the rose predominating upon blue, orange-yellow,
and rose-pink ground. Green webbed borders. Similar rugs are in
the Royal Palace at Madrid.   *Size, 14 feet 1 inch x 9 feet 6 inches*

[SEE ILLUSTRATION]

124

423 **LONG STRIP OF BLUE AND SILVER SILK BROCADE**
SPANISH, 18TH CENTURY
With sky-blue ground sustaining a pleasing design of naturalistic flower arabesques and stripes in silver thread.
Length about 17 feet; width, 21 inches

424 **PAIR OF FIGURED CRIMSON SILK DAMASK PORTIERES**
SPANISH, 18TH CENTURY
Patterned with rocaille scrolls and flowers and trimmed with cut silk fringe. (2)
Size of each, 8 feet x 7 feet

425 **PANEL OF FIGURED CRIMSON SILK DAMASK**
SPANISH, 18TH CENTURY
Patterned with large pomegranates and leaves. Consisting of four strips of about two and a half yards each.

426 **ANTIQUE APULJARRAS RUG**
Bright mustard-yellow ground, sustaining conventionalized floral medallions in deep blue and green.
Size, 9 feet x 5 feet

427 **PANEL OF FIGURED CRIMSON SILK DAMASK**
SPANISH, 18TH CENTURY
Composed of four strips, totalling about eleven yards.

428 **FIGURED CRIMSON SILK DAMASK LONG POINTED VALANCE**
SPANISH, 18TH CENTURY
Trimmed with silk tassels. Matching the preceding.
Length about 18 feet; depth, 10 inches

429 **PANEL OF GREEN SILK DAMASK** SPANISH, 18TH CENTURY
With all-over flower design in two shades of jade-green.
Size about 5 feet 6 inches x 7 feet

430 **SILK BROCADE CHASUBLE** SPANISH, 18TH CENTURY
With rich floral design in soft green and white on rose ground.

431 **TWO FLOWERED SILK SAINTS' ROBES**
SPANISH, 18TH CENTURY
Triangular small cloaks with rich flower and scroll design in colors on dark ground. Gold thread collars. (2)

432 BLUE SILK CAPE   SPANISH, EARLY 18TH CENTURY
Designed with sprays of flowers in pale yellow. Gold galloon.
Size, 50 x 23 inches

433 NEEDLEWORK PANEL OF THE LOUIS XVI PERIOD
         FRENCH, LATE 18TH CENTURY
Designed with trophies framed by floral wreaths in colored silk petit-
point needlework.   *Size, 23 x 21 inches*

434 TWO EMBROIDERED VELVET PRIEST'S COLLARS
         SPANISH, 16TH CENTURY
Ruby velvet with appliquéd silk embroidery of papal tiara and floral
arabesques. (2)   *Width, 23 inches*

435 RUBY-RED VELVET TABLE MAT   SPANISH, 17TH CENTURY
With gold braid border.   *Size, 28½ x 20 inches*

436 TWO CUSHIONS
Covered in seventeenth century crimson velvet, one with gold ap-
pliquéd corners, the other piped in yellow. (2)
Size about 19 x 13 inches

437 TWO EMBROIDERED RED VELVET CHAIR SEATS
         SPANISH, 18TH CENTURY
Rich design of bold floral arabesques embroidered in bright colored
silks on a ruby velvet ground. Embroidery of later date. (2)
Size about 23 x 21 inches

438 THREE EMBROIDERED RED VELVET CHAIR SEATS
         SPANISH, 17TH CENTURY
Similar to the preceding. (2)   *Size about 23 x 21 inches*

439 PANEL OF FLOWERED GREEN SILK DAMASK
         SPANISH, 18TH CENTURY
Size about 9 feet x 3 feet 6 inches

440 TWO PAIRS OF FLOWERED CHINTZ CURTAINS
Pleasing "Queen Anne" design of rose and leaf sprays in delicate
red and blue on white. Buff lining. (4)
Length about 7 feet; width about 3 feet

441 **PAIR OF CHINTZ CURTAINS**
With all-over pattern of iris flowers and leaves in colors. (2)
Length about 9 feet; width about 6 feet

442 **PAIR OF GLAZED CHINTZ CURTAINS**
Patterned with exotic flowers and bunches of berries in rose colors
on pale green. (2)   *Length about 7 feet; width about 6 feet*

443 **THREE OLD FLOWER-PRINTED AND PLEATED LINEN
DAMASK VALANCES**
Patterned with sprays of carnations in rose colors. Charming de-
sign. (3) ·   *Length about 6 feet*

444 **PAIR OF FLOWERED CHINTZ CURTAINS**
Patterned with large semi-conventionalized iris flowers and leaves
in rose and turquoise on white. (2)
Length about 10 feet; width about 4 feet

445 **PAIR OF FLOWERED CHINTZ CURTAINS**
Patterned with detached sprays of roses on dotted white ground.
Reverse with blue flowers. (2)
Length about 6 feet 6 inches; width about 4 feet 6 inches

446 **TWO FLOWERED CHINTZ LONG CURTAINS AND TWO
VALANCES**
Patterned with sprays of roses. One curtain and two valances
glazed. (4)

This catalogue designed by The Anderson Galleries
Half-tone plates by Walker Engraving Company
Composition and press-work by
Publishers Printing Company, New York
Binding by The Trade Bindery Inc.

CPSIA information can be obtained
at www.ICGtesting.com
Printed in the USA
BVHW041941300122
627572BV00011B/624

9 781014 702685